Huntin' Camp Tales

Stories, Tips and Humor

Edited by
Mike Vail

North American Hunting Club
Minneapolis, Minnesota

Acknowledgements

We would like to thank the following for their help:

NAHC Members, for sharing their exciting and humorous hunting experiences. These pages will be sure to enhance your hunting season.

Product Development Manager **Jeff Boehler** for his hard work in coordinating this book project.

Cartoonists **Joseph Columbus, John Fitzgerald, David Harbaugh, Harry Nelson, Richard Stubler,** and **Richard Tomasic** for their humorous look at hunting through their hilarious cartoons. They will surely tickle the funny bone of NAHC Members.

Cover photo copyright © David R. Stoecklein Photography
Book design and layout by Teresa Marrone

ISBN 0-914697-80-3
3 4 5 6 / 02 01 00 99

Table of Contents

Introduction

Bill Miller–Executive Director, North American Hunting Club

Quotations that live forever in infamy are created every year in hunting camp. One of the greats I remember from the "Waldo Gang Camp" of which I was a part in my youth was uttered by one of the senior statesmen as he stepped through the tent flap with even more than his usual flourish. A snow storm was raging outside, and in the moment before the overpowering heat from the oil stove began to melt the accumulated flakes from his stocking cap and collar he uttered the immortal words, "Gentlemen, after these many years experience, I can tell you for certain that the three most important things not to lose when answering nature's call in the woods are: your car keys, your billfold and...your balance!"

Truly—words to live by!

Such sharpness of wit and depth of thought are not easily come by! Unprodded and unchallenged, few of us would ever reach such pinnacles of wisdom! Oft said, but of far less inspired origin is the platitude, "You can't grow beautiful flowers without a lot of fertilizer."

Well, the book you've got in your hands is "the fertilizer." It's up to you to make beautiful things grow from it. It shouldn't be difficult. There's enough rich, mixed compost here to grow a forest of deep thoughts and diabolical schemes in any NAHC member's noggin. We're just proud we could provide the shovel.

Oh ya, before you undertake this enjoyment, heed one warning. Don't forget to look up from its pages once in a while to see if a buck or a bull has blundered into view.

Enjoy.

Bill Miller
Executive Director

A Hunter's Pledge

Responsible hunting provides unique challenges and rewards. However, the future of the sport depends on each hunter's behavior and ethics. Therefore, as a hunter, I pledge to:

- Respect the environment and wildlife.

- Respect property and landowners.

- Show consideration for non-hunters.

- Hunt safely. Know and obey the law.

- Support wildlife and habitat conservation.

- Pass on an ethical hunting tradition.

- Strive to improve my outdoor skills and understanding of wildlife.

- Hunt only with ethical hunters.

By following these principles of conduct each time I go afield, I will give my best to the sport, the public, the environment and myself. The responsibility to hunt ethically is mine; the future of hunting depends on me.

Your Hunting Dollar

The Wildlife Conservation programs of state Fish and Game departments add up to a vast undertaking, one involving thousands of people working for the well-being of hundreds of species of birds, animals and fish, game and non-game species alike, on millions of acres of land and water.

This costs a tremendous amount of money, hundreds of millions of dollars every year. Here, once again, the hunter enters the picture, because unlike other state governmental agencies, fish and game departments receive little support from taxes paid by the general public. Instead, virtually all their operating funds come from the outdoor fraternity of hunters and fishermen.

This means that hunters and fishermen are paying, as they have for many years, almost all of the bills for practical wildlife conservation and paying them not just for their own benefit, but for the benefit of all Americans.

Hunters alone, dating as far back as the 1920s, have paid the lion's share for conservation.

The knowledge of how this money is gathered and how it is spent for the benefit of wildlife contributes greatly to an understanding of the overall conservation picture, and the hunter's important relationship to it.

Nelson

"How can you have bagged your deer?
I haven't finished unloading the car yet!"

Keep It Simple

You can cram your mind so full of great things gleaned from seminars and conversations and magazines and videos, that they're impossible to sort out. You know of so many options you mentally paralyze yourself

The only solution is to go back to basics: Animals need to eat, remain safe and as comfortable as possible, and reproduce their species. They need to move around to accomplish these things. Various factors affect how and what they do, and when they do it.

That's all there is…plus paying attention to the wind at all times.

Hunting Trip Checklist

The Hunting Trip Checklist on the following pages (pages 12 and 13) will help you prepare for your upcoming hunts and eliminate those last-minute scrambles as you gather your gear. Each column covers a trip (12 in all).

Start by writing the date of your trip in the top box. You can easily prepare for two or more trips at a time. Many of the major items you'll want to take along are already listed and you can write in others to fit your own needs.

For example, in the "Weapons and Ammo" area, you might fill it out like this:

Hunting Trip Checklist

Trip Date:	3-25	9-15	9-30	10-11	11-5							
Weapons and Ammo												
Firearms Rifle 1 *Browning BAR*		✔		✔								
Rifle 2 *Thompson 30-06*			✔	✔								
Rifle 3 *Rem. .22*				✔								
Shotgun 1 *Rem. 1100*	✔											
Shotgun 2												
Handgun 1 *Browning .22*	✔	✔		✔								
Handgun 2 *S&W .44*			✔									
Ammo Gun 1 *.270 Win.*		✔		✔								
Gun 2 *Federal 30-06*			✔	✔								
Gun 3 *12 ga. 3-1/2*	✔											
Gun 4 *.22 Longs*	✔	✔	✔	✔								

You can enter other items in the blanks, too, or change an item to suite your own needs.

With this system, you'll never again get to camp and realize you forgot something important. Enjoy your hunt!

The Checklist starts on the next page ➡

Hunting Trip Checklist

	Trip Date:														

Weapons and Ammo

Firearms	Rifle 1															
	Rifle 2															
	Rifle 3															
	Shotgun 1															
	Shotgun 2															
	Handgun 1															
	Handgun 2															
Ammo	Gun 1															
	Gun 2															
	Gun 3															
	Gun 4															
Gun Gear	Cleaning Kit															
	Bore Sighter															
	Scope															
	Choke Tubes															
	Sling															
	Belt/Cartridge Case															
	Gun Case															
Bow & Gear	Bow 1															
	Bow 2															
	Arrows															
	Target Points															
	Broadheads															
	Broadhead Cement															
	Extra String															
	Release															
	String Wax															

Big Game Gear

Binoculars															
Spotting Scope															
Bone Saw															
Skinning Knife															
Scents/Lures															
Drag Line/Rope															
Trail Timer															
Portable Tree Stand															
Field Dressing Gloves															

Waterfowl & Upland Bird Gear

Calls															
Decoys															
Hip Boots/Waders															
Identification Charts															
Portable Blind															
Flotation Suit/Devices															
Seats/Cushions															
Vest															

Trip Date:													

Field Equipment

License/Tags													
Regulations													
Compass													
Range Finder													
Topo Maps													
Survival Kit													

Camping Gear

Tent													
Stove and Fuel													
Cooler													
Sleeping Bags													
Lantern and Fuel													
Axe													
Sharpening Stone													
Towel													

Personal Items

Miscellaneous

Alarm Clock													
Pocket Knife													
Sewing Kit													
Hearing Protectors													
Fanny Pack													
Back Pack													
Sunscreen													
Insect Repellent													
Watch													

Clothing

Jacket/Parka													
Camo Outfit													
Insulated Underwear													
Rain Gear													
Boots													
Headgear													
Gloves													
Suspenders													
Wool Socks													

Other Gear

Road Maps													
First Aid Kit													
Flashlight and Batteries													
Camera and Film													
Portable Radio													
Fishing Rod and Tackle													
Toilet Paper													
Groceries/Food Supplies													
Bandana													
Thermos													

"I don't like the looks of this..."

Recovering Big Game

Mark LaBarbera

The old adage, "You can't cook it if you don't shoot it," is missing one step. After you shoot it, you have to find it. As Uncle Ignazino LaBarbera would tell us younger hunters years ago, "Tracks make thin soup. You boys better get on that deer's trail if you want to eat tonight."

Iggy and his brother Giuseppe shared some trailing tips back then that have proven effective over the years. For some of you, the tips in this big game recovery guide may be new. For others, some of them will be old hat. Consider it, then, a refresher course.

Whether you hunt with rifle, bow, handgun or muzzle-loader, shots at game should be calculated. Sometimes that calculation comes as a snap decision as the huge buck busts out of brush yards ahead of you, but the decision to shoot or not to shoot must be made. We owe it to our-selves, the sport and the game to take shots that dispatch game quickly and cleanly.

When you connect on your target and it doesn't drop in sight, the animal should be trailed until it is found or until you are sure that it was not mortally hit. After a hit, follow the steps below.

1 Sit tight. Watch where the game goes until it's out of sight, but also make sure you pin-point the spot where the animal was standing when you shot. Also, try to picture how the animal reacted when you shot.

2 Note your position since many hunters forget where they were when they shot. And pick out a specific landmark to help you remember where the game was last seen. Note the time before leaving your stand.

3 But don't let anxiety overcome you. Over-anxious hunters push game that may have otherwise stayed nearby to die. Veteran hunters recommend waiting one hour, and at least twice that long, for a gut shot, but you'll have to judge what's appropriate for your situation. Hunting on public land, near major roadways and in an

continued on page 16

area with heavy hunting pressure or hungry predators may force you to pursue your animal sooner.

4 When it's time to move, go first to where you shot. Check for blood, hair or other signs. Bowhunters can look for their arrow.

5 Follow any blood sign or obvious trails the game left. If none, follow the path you recall the animal taking toward where you last saw it.

6 Mark the beginning of the trail with flagging or toilet paper, but remember to come back later and remove this from the woods. No sense leaving an unsightly indication of your presence or, for that matter, no sense letting anyone else know you had shooting. When you're concentrating on the trail, these markers often keep you from losing your sense of direction.

7 If blood sign is scarce, leave a marker at the last visible sign. Pay attention to whether the blood is dark (liver or kidney hit), bubbly and pinkish (lung or neck arteries and windpipe hit) or greenish mixed with partially digested food (gut hit).

8 Walk to the side of the trail so you don't disturb it. You may need to go back and check the last sign or tracks.

9 From the last blood beyond where you last saw the animal, if there is no other sign, follow game trails for at least one-quarter mile. Move silently towards clumps of brush and windfalls where game may hide. Generally, wounded game will move downhill, so let your feet take you where the animal might have gone when all other sign has disappeared.

10 If you're trailing with a companion, move quietly, one man watching ahead and to the sides, while the other checks for sign.

11 If no blood or sign shows up again for some distance, check obvious crossings at stream banks, human trails and barbed wire fence openings.

12 On cool days when you run out of daylight, resume tracking in the morning; you may be surprised to find a stiff animal. If you're worried about coyotes, dogs or bears, or warm-weather meat spoilage, use a lantern for night trailing when the blood's phosphorous sparkles.

13 Finally, you'll often find your trophy if you look specifically for it, rather than scanning the entire landscape expecting the animal to pop out of the background. On big game, white undersides and antlers can be picked out. With bears, heavy dark spots stand out more than shadows. Brushy areas filter light, so an unusually consistent dark spot could give away your bear's presence.

If you follow these guidelines you will likely recover your game and you will have exercised every option short of heat-seeking sensors to find your trophy.

Use Binoculars

Any hunter who takes his deer hunting seriously will invest in a pair of quality binoculars and use them regularly. Hunters have spotted many deer with their binoculars, particularly during periods of low light, such as early in the morning or toward sunset. Binoculars are especially handy when hunting around large agricultural fields.

·THE GREAT·
Whitetail Quiz

Grab a pen, sit back and test your knowledge of this most popular big game animal. This colorful quiz was prepared by Al Hofacker, vice president of The Stump Sitters Deer Study Group, which is dedicated to the study and dissemination of information about the white-tail. Feeling like a white-tail know-it-all? Try your luck on the other parts of the quiz; you'll find them throughout the book! Part Two is on pages 44-45.

1) Male white-tailed deer grow:
    A. Antlers
    B. Horns

2) What is the difference between antlers and horns?
    A. There is no difference. The terms "antlers" and
       "horns" are interchangeable.
    B. Antlers are shed annually, but horns are not.
    C. Horns grow much faster than antlers.

3) The bases of a whitetail's antlers are located:
    A. In front of the ears.
    B. Behind the ears.

4) Antler growth is triggered by:
    A. The age of deer.
    B. Winter severity.
    C. Food availability.
    D. Photoperiodism.

5) The age of a buck can be determined by:
    A. Measuring the length of the antler's main beam.
    B. Counting the number of antler points.
    C. Measuring the diameter of the antler near its base.
    D. None of the above.

6) Maximum antler growth usually occurs when the buck is:
   A. 1.5 to 3.5 years old.
   B. 4.5 to 6.5 years old.
   C. 7.5 to 9.5 years old.
   D. 10.5 years or older.

7) The size of a buck's rack is usually determined by:
   A. Genetics and nutrition.
   B. Age only.
   C. Climate.

8) The "stain" or color of a buck's rack is determined by:
   A. The amount and quality of food eaten while the antlers are growing.
   B. The age of the buck.
   C. The amount of hemoglobin supplied to the antlers during growth.
   D. The type of vegetation rubbed during the rut.

9) The basic shape of a buck's rack is:
   A. Basically the same each year, but larger.
   B. Larger each year with different shapes.
   C. Basically the same each year until the prime of life and then there is a decline in size.

10) The gestation period of the white-tailed doe is approximately:
    A. 150 days.
    B. 200 days.
    C. 250 days.

11) Adult does usually give birth to:
    A. A single fawn.
    B. Twin fawns.
    C. Triplets.

12) At birth a fawn weighs approximately:
    A. Four to eight pounds.
    B. 10 to 15 pounds.
    C. 20 to 25 pounds.

Answers are on page 184.

Match Point

James Potter, Harrisville, Michigan

November 15 of this year's deer season found the same 15 or 16 of us gathered for the opening day hunt a mile or so north of my hometown, Harrisville, Michigan. We enjoyed seeing a lot of deer that day, but, as deer tend to do, they held the upper hand and we could account for only one small three-pointer at day's end.

The second day, however, was a bit more productive as a spike, six-pointer and a crop horn eight-point buck were taken by noon. The latter was taken by my father, Forrest Potter. He had spent most of the morning sitting, so he decided to try a slow walk along what he calls a "hogback" ridge. Halfway down this particular ridge, he saw a buck ambling up the hill toward him. The buck held his head right to the ground. My father had a harder time dragging that deer the quarter mile to my truck than he did shooting it. By noon, he knew he'd spend the afternoon recuperating at home.

My brother and I returned to the woods around 2:30 but had not quite arrived at our usual spot when I glanced down a ravine to see two deer feeding on wintergreen. It didn't take long for me to stop the truck, uncase the gun, and put the scope on them. Convinced that I could see a spike, I had Gil check them out and, even though he couldn't say that he witnessed what I did, I stayed behind as he motored further into the woods.

I eased back in about 100 feet from those two deer and just watched for about 20 minutes when, suddenly, I heard something off to my left. It was Gil who had returned to check out the deer. He had said he would go check out Dad's lucky spot. He had no time to move, though, because from out of that ravine the four-pointer took off behind me. I swung on him, making sure I was safely away from Gil, and touched the gun off, taking him just behind the front shoulder. When he didn't slow down, I shot again just as he entered some large pines, and down he went. Both bullets entered the same hole but exited two inches apart. My deer was taken about 400 yards from where dad took his deer.

We made short work of dressing and dragging out the deer.

As we do with all bucks we get, I removed the antlers to mount them on a wooden plaque. Well, when I got Dad's and mine home and began working on the skulls, found a small tip of an antler embedded in the skull of my deer. Thinking that a bit odd, you can imagine how very odd it became when I noticed that same amount of horn missing from my dad's trophy. I took that broken tip and right before my unbelieving eyes, discovered a perfect match of the two pieces.

I've often wondered what the odds of this rarity are, but especially how rare when you consider it was discovered by this father and son combo on exactly the same day.

How to Smell Like a Tree

Before the hunt, put your hunting clothes and boots in a large plastic bag with some crushed leaves, broken branches or other type of vegetation native to the area you will be hunting. The escaping plant odors will give your clothes the right smell.

About Moose

The regal moose is an animal that you'll be very lucky to see in the wild. Although there are about 400,000 on the North American continent, you won't find them along the fields near home— unless you happen to live near a fairly remote field! The moose looks like an animal designed by committee, but they are actually quite graceful for the largest antlered species on the planet.

- During the rut in the far North, bulls have been known to battle trains! That would obviously not be a good time to run into one face-to-face.
- Bull moose can grow to heights of ten feet to the tops of their antlers.
- Their antlers can be over 6 feet wide and weigh over 90 pounds.
- Moose are actually the world's largest deer—and the largest North American game species.
- Moose will stand chest deep in water and submerge their heads to "graze" on bottom growing plants.
- In a trot, a moose can travel at 35 miles per hour and can add another 10 m.p.h. in a full gallop.

No matter what kind of knife you prefer—folding, lockback, fixed blade or pocket model—it's best to select one with a handle of either wood or textured plastic. Metal and other smooth handles are difficult to handle when wet or covered with blood.

Knife Makers Word Search

```
U K C U B S W E S T E R N E G
C A N O T G N I M E R R E K R
W H R W E N H A F R O S T C O
N K E A S P Y D E R C O D A H
C R K H E S A C L I V N W J M
A A O S T G Y L O I U I R K A
M M B R K I A N C I N F E C N
I H U E C K M T S C E C G A E
L C S K O G O B H H A O E L D
L N R T P R M E E P E L R B A
U E A N I I S R U R N O B G R
S B S N T T O M A E L N E N H
S S O P E A A R I E N I R G S
L X B R O W N I N G B A N Y B
E S A S E L B R A M F L E E C
```

BEAR MGC	COLONIAL	REMINGTON
BENCHMARK	FROST	SHRADE
BLACKJACK	GERBER	SPYDERCO
BOKER	GROHMAN	TIMBERLINE
BROWNING	KERSHAW	VICTORINOX
BUCK	LAKOTA	WESTERN
CAMILLUS	MARBLES	WINCHESTER
CASE	PUMA	

Answers are on page 186.

"The Hunting Family" Has Special Meaning To The Bucks

By Charles T. "Chuck" Buck, President of Buck Knives, Inc.

When we talk about family at "Buck" Knives, the word carries a lot of special meaning for us. Every one of the good people who work with us are a part of the Buck Family, in a very, real sense.

But to me, family is a very personal matter, too. I learned how to make knives from my dad, Al, who is chairman of the board. He learned his knifemaking skills from his father, H.H Buck. It was Grandpa, of course, who started it all back at the turn of the century. He thought we could make a *better* knife... and he did! We work hard at accomplishing that same goal today.

My son, Chuck Jr., is a key part of our management team now, and we're waiting for his two-year-old son, Josh, to grow up just a little more so we can pass on the knifemaking skills to our fifth generation.

The outdoors is a big part of our lives, too. One of our favorite projects is the "Buck Grand Slam." Our goal is to bag one North American Buck each year.

My son and I take part in these annual hunts, accompanied by four outdoor writers and professional guides. New Buck products are used by all participants, so it provides a great field test and instant feedback.

In November, 1984 we went to Saratoga, Wyoming in search of pronghorn antelope. Both of us scored, and Chuck Jr. had the better trophy of the two.

Mule deer were the target in November, 1985 in Montana. Again we both scored, and Chuck Jr. had the best trophy of the hunt.

Last year, I must confess, we were both blanked in our quest for blacktail on Queen Charlotte Islands in Canada, but the family honor was upheld by my son-in-law Joe Houser, who was on his first hunt.

Family togetherness—in the outdoors, in our business lives and in our commitment to God—is the Buck keystone.

Charles T. Buck
President–Buck Knives, Inc.

Dutch Oven Quail

Serves: 4 to 6
Prep Time: 2 hours

6–8 dressed quail
⅓ cup olive oil or butter
2 cloves garlic, minced
  (or garlic salt)
1 medium-sized onion,
  minced
¾ cup chopped parsley
½ cup chopped green
  pepper
¾ cup sauterne or
  other white wine
1 cup (or can) mushrooms
2 cans (8 oz) tomato sauce
  Pinch of thyme
  Pinch of rosemary
  Salt and pepper to taste

Heat oil or butter in hot Dutch oven. Fry birds to red brown color all over, turning frequently to assure even heating. Add garlic, onion, parsley and green pepper, fry until tender and golden; then add the wine and cover. Lower heat to simmer. A few minutes later, add tomato sauce, mushrooms and seasoning. Continue to simmer for approximately 1½ hours. Serve over rice or noodles.

The story of Buck Knives, one of the world's largest producers of quality knives, reads like a classic American success story.

Charles T. (Chuck) Buck, president of the California corporation, represents the third generation of the Buck family to head the firm. His grandfather, the late H.H. Buck, handcrafted the first Buck knives at the turn of the century.

Chuck began working in the family business as a young boy, preparing worn–out files which his father would hollow grind and shape into tempered knife blades.

Today, Buck Knives' new manufacturing facility and corporate headquarters encompasses more than four acres under one roof. Despite tremendous growth and modern technology, the Buck family still pursues the original goal set by "Grandpa" Buck—to make a better knife.

While hunting deer in the X-1 zone of northern California we saw the strangest thing. We had staked out a brushy area near a small pond, hoping to ambush deer. While waiting, we saw a chipmunk trying to reach the end of a branch overhanging the deep end of the pond. Before we knew it a largemouth bass broke water and took the chipmunk right off the branch. We looked at each other and decided the hunt was over for the moment. We dashed for camp and gathered what little fishing tackle we had.

We began to sneak up on the pond, and once in sight, we couldn't believe our eyes. There was the largemouth putting another acorn on the end of the branch!

–Life Member Bill Alfaro,
Livermore CA

"...Your hunting dogs aren't dependents..."

Animal Match-Ups

Match the description of an animal at the right to one of the names below.

Whitetail Deer

Wild Turkey

Woodcock

Bighorn Sheep

Squirrel

Ruffed Grouse

Black Bear

Canvasback

Ring-Necked Pheasant

Canada Goose

Caribou

Antelope

Blue-Winged Teal

Javelina

Elk

Moose

Answers on page 186

1. This 300-350 pound herd animal has a distinctive creamy white rump patch. You must be in shape and unafraid of heights when going after this trophy.

2. Not a finicky eater, this 250 pound loner is the heaviest in the fall, leanest in the spring.

3. Probably the most migratory of all big game animals, this magnificent creature actually carries "shovels" on its head.

4. Although you may be able to spot this animal from great distances, it is challenging to hunt. It possesses extremely keen eyesight and can run as fast as 50 miles per hour.

5. Among the earliest ducks to fly south every fall, this small "speed demon" presents a difficult target to the hunter.

6. At home in the deserts of southwestern United States and Mexico, this small, dark mammal obtains water by eating succulent desert plants or frequenting water holes where available.

7. Due to modern conservation and transplanting techniques,this very large game bird is hunted in most states in the nation.

8. When challenging another suitor during the mating ritual, this impressive mammal uses a unique "bugle" sound.

9. The largest member of the deer family in North America.

10. Introduced in to the U.S. from Asia, this popular game bird occupies much of the corn and grain region of the United States.

11. This woodland bird gets its name from the dark feathers on each side of its neck.

12. Thought to be the fastest of our ducks, a tight group of these large ducks resembles a squadron of jet fighters as they fly over larger bodies of water.

13. This little migrating game bird prefers forests and is fondly nicknamed "timberdoodle."

14. Found in virtually all North American tree regions, this small animal is a favorite for young hunters.

15. This large waterfowl bird can be easily identified by its "honking" and "V" shaped flocks.

16. This magnificent animal is hunted by more North American Hunting Club Members than any other big game species.

In The Dark Of A Bear Chase

Judd Cooney

Jerry and Sharron are the type of clients guides dream
about booking. They come to the hunt full of infectious
enthusiasm and every day of the hunt they get more
excited. When they talk about being together, they mean
together, whether it is going to a football game or sitting in
the same tree stand waiting for a bear.

A pine squirrel visiting the bear bait to snatch a bite to
eat aroused their excitement, so it was only natural that the
gorgeous blonde bear that strolled into the small clearing
really got their fires lit!

The tree stand in which they were sitting was one of my
deluxe, permanent stands that is big enough for several
people. Jerry was standing behind Sharron with the camera,
ready to photograph her arrowing the bear. The bear didn't
take long to get in the right position, and Sharron took even
less time to get an arrow from her compound into the bear.

Instead of heading for the heavy timber in a blur like
arrow-hit bears are supposed to, this bear jumped onto the
tree by the bait, bawling and growling. He climbed up
about 10 feet. He then jumped out of that tree and took to
the one next to it, somewhat closer to the tree stand and
repeated his act. All Jerry and Sharron could think was that
she had really made the bear mad and he was looking for
them. Jerry dropped the camera and tried to get his handgun
out, only to see the bear finally disappear into the woods.

By the time I got to them, just after dark, they were
about as hyper as two bowhunters could be. After
hearing the story, I tried to pick up the blood trail,
but could find very little to follow. In situations like this,
I don't fool around; I have a couple of four-legged blood
trailers that have saved losing countless wounded bears
and can blood trail in the dark a lot faster than I can.

It didn't take me long to get my two top Plott hounds, a
couple of eager, young dogs and one of my guides on the
three-hour-old blood trail. The dogs milled around where

the bear was hit and then took off up a rocky ridge in pursuit. The plan was that I would follow the dogs and stay within hearing distance while my guide would keep my light in sight and watch out for Jerry and Sharron. As the chase progressed, the bear headed into some steep, oak-covered canyons and made a wide circle heading back toward the bait site.

continued on page 30

Jerry and Sharron were struggling up and down the canyons in the dark, cussing bears, outfitters and oak brush that grabs everything that gets near it. They didn't realize the guide up ahead was keeping light in sight and staying just far enough ahead to keep me in sight and the dogs in hearing. They had visions of spending the rest of the night wandering around, lost in the dark, so they were about to kill themselves trying to make time in the damnable oak brush and rocky slopes.

They were floundering up one particularly rugged, oak-covered slope with Jerry leading the way. He had Sharron's bow in one hand and the flashlight in the other. Sharron was hanging on to Jerry's belt to keep from sliding back down the slope.

Suddenly, Jerry let out a gasp and told Sharron not to make a sound. His gasping breaths and burning lungs were trying to extract the last bit of precious oxygen from the thin mountain air when he heard brush breaking just ahead of them. The wounded bear had obviously circled and was back-trailing himself right into their laps!

Jerry whispered for Sharron to hold tight as he dropped her bow and grabbed for a solid handhold on an oak limb. The snuffling animal breaking brush was almost on top of them so Jerry did the only thing he could to protect Sharron and himself. He grabbed the .357 Mag. on his hip! In order to get a hold on the pistol he had to let go of his flashlight, which rolled down the hill into the thick oakbrush.

This left them both hanging precariously from the limber oak bush, on the steep slope, with no footing, in the pitch black. Not the best of situations when you are about to be run over by a wounded bear. Jerry thought that by keeping quiet the bear might pass them in the dark, but suddenly it was on him. The furred nemesis hit him smack in the chest, almost making him lose his grip and sending them all tumbling into the canyon.

Fortunately, before he could get a shot off from his .357 Mag. in self-defense, Troubles, one of my young hounds, licked Jerry right in the face, and thereby saved his own life!

Once Jerry and Sharron got their tongues unstuck from their gullets and their hearts out of their throats, both of them and their new-found friend struggled to the top of the hill to continue the chase.

The dogs had trailed the bear nearly back to the bait before they treed it in a Ponderosa pine. Jerry and Sharron were almost back to normal by the time they found me, sitting under a nearby tree, contemplating the lot of outfitters in general and me in particular. As they plopped down in the pine duff by me I casually asked, "Sharron, what color was the bear you hit?"

"Oh, it was a gorgeous pale blonde that almost glowed when it walked up to the bait barrel," she bubbled with her normal enthusiasm.

Without saying a word, I turned my powerful light into the branches of the tree 30 feet above the bawling, baying hounds and lit up the good-sized *black* bear perched comfortably on the limb. Somewhere those two blankety-blank bears had switched places and we had chased and treed the wrong bear!

continued on page 32

In The Dark Of A Bear Chase
continued from page 31

We left the bear and tried to get the dogs back on the trail without success: they knew where the bear was and weren't about to leave it alone.

Later, Jerry's photo showed Sharron's hit to be high on the shoulder with little penetration. Within a week the "gorgeous" sneaky, double-dealing, blonde bear was back on the bait, eating free groceries and Jerry and Sharron were back home, regaling their neighbors with tales of bears attacking in the dark of the Colorado night.

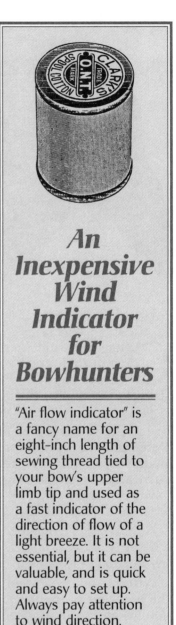

An Inexpensive Wind Indicator for Bowhunters

"Air flow indicator" is a fancy name for an eight-inch length of sewing thread tied to your bow's upper limb tip and used as a fast indicator of the direction of flow of a light breeze. It is not essential, but it can be valuable, and is quick and easy to set up. Always pay attention to wind direction.

— R.STUBLER —

"Get ready, Frank, we're going to see some action."

All About Deer

ACROSS
1. Trophy
5. Glass part of scope
7. Needed for float hunting
8. Male of various mammals
10. Large antler pairs
12. Result of a good shot
14. Not down
16. Field dress a deer
17. Crazy
18. A quick look
21. Who's going hunting
22. Solid deciduous growth
25. Rooster on the barn
27. Voice of a bird
28. Two equal results
29. Consumed food
31. To move rapidly
33. Short for crowlike bird

34. Prey on other creatures
36. What bucks and does do
37. Travel to
39. Triumphs in a contest
41. Bow shooting practice
42. Abilities
43. Semisolid material
45. Several young deer
46. Buck activity during rut
47. Western deer species

DOWN
1. Where deer hang out
2. Swells on rutting buck
3. Deer walking pattern
4. To jump
6. Odor
9. Alive and _____
10. Deer hindquarters
11. Indicates presence of deer

13. Hooked to deer's shoulder
15. Soft antler tissue
19. Protected side of a hill
21. Gland on deer's leg
22. Short word
23. Material to make slugs
24. Deer's mating period
26. Nothing
27. Adult male deer
28. Gland on a deer's leg
30. Female sheep
31. Part of deer's back foot
32. Uncooked
35. Another small word
38. Tree in good deer woods
40. Animal droppings
42. To be on stand
44. Deer sensory organ

Answers on page 187.

Shelly's First Hunt

Cory Duncan

NAHC
Staff Story

Here's a quick version of a hunting story I tell friends and family about one of the reasons that brought my wife and I together.

While attending the University of North Dakota in 1990 I was a duck/goose fanatic with academics far down on my list of priorities. Shelly, my new girlfriend at the time and now my wife, came to visit and of course had to go hunting. She was surprised when we had to get up at 3:30 and drive over an hour to hunt, and also surprised when we had to walk over a mile to the hunting spot. She tried her best to put on some makeup and look good for the ducks, geese, mosquitoes, rain, wind, chest-high grass, mud, and other obstacles.

After a morning of standing around in miserable conditions without any action, she was wondering why she was where she was. Shelly was also learning that drinking a lot of coffee while out away from a bathroom was not a good idea, and was hunkered down in the brush about 50 yards from me for the third or fourth time of the morning. A flock of geese decided to pay our barley field a visit and came within range. The shot rang out and I heard Shelly scream as she thought I had shot at her. With that goose 40–50 yards in the air it took a couple seconds before coming down with a thud about a foot in front of her and then I heard another scream. That was Shelly's first day of hunting...

"The rest of the flock is due in just after ten a.m. out of the northwest; now, where's my corn?"

Woods Wisdom

A wise old hunter once said, "When answering nature's call in the woods, the three most important things not to lose are your car keys, your billfold and your balance."

Honker Math

Two duck hunters were spending some slow time in the blind watching seemingly endless "Vs" of migrating Canadian honkers far above their heads. After a while, one hunter said to the other, "Why do you suppose that one side of the "V" is longer than the other? "The other hunter considered the different possibilities and finally said "I think it's because there are more geese on one side than the other!"

Good for the Soul

Like the boy who goes from bicycle to car, a hunter goes from rabbits and squirrels to other game. These are the most popular small-game animals across the country, and they provide some of the best hunting experiences for man and boy.

Small-game hunting, with the sweet delectability of success, engrains itself and nestles in the hunter's heart at a young age. It lures him back frequently to the fields and woods of earlier days in search of rabbits and squirrels.

Like the healthy man who returns to the bicycle for exercise, many veteran hunters return to the basics of small game hunting. Peaceful afternoons in a squirrel woods refresh the soul.

Don't Give Up Early
Steve Binning, Cincinnati, Ohio

Bow hunting season is a special time for me especially early in the season—opening day to be exact. In my hunting area the rut usually does not start this early and it seems that the bucks are a little finicky at this time of the year.

I was hunting from a tree stand one morning early in the season and I was using the rattling technique to try and draw in some bucks. I had a grunt call with me but I figured it was too early in the season to use it.

I positioned my stand on a trail where another intersecting trail was going away from me. It was getting late in the morning, about eleven o'clock, and I was about to give it up. I had been up in that stand all morning and had not seen a thing moving. Then on the other trail I saw movement; it was an eight-point buck moving slow and unalarmed. I sat there and watched and hoped that he would hit the trail I was sitting on, but he didn't; he was moving away from me and I was trying to think of something to get his attention and get him to hit the trail I was sitting on.

I decided to try my grunt call. I made three short grunts and stopped and watched. The buck stopped for a moment then started to walk away. I gave three more short grunts and stopped and watched. The buck was about out of my sight. I watched in surprise as the buck turned around on the other trail and was heading back toward the trail I was sitting on.

The buck came within twenty yards of my stand; now he was very curious, smelling and listening and trying to locate and identify where the grunt came from. I was so excited when I took aim I hit a clump of leaves and spooked the deer, but I have tried this method several times and it does seem to work. So the next time you find that the deer are out of range and are finicky try the three grunt method—the deer's curious nature is too much.

36

"Is that all you ever think about--how long 'till mating season?"

The "Bear Necessities"

You'll want to pay attention when you find these tracks in the field. Can you name them?

Answers are on page 189.

By The Numbers

According to the Wildlife Management Institute...

✔ Between 1979–1989, hunters bagged 1,363,903 pronghorns in 18 states and provinces in North America.

✔ Whitetail deer hunters can annually take 30% or up to one-third of the population without reducing the herd or causing a population decrease.

According to the US Fish and Wildlife Service...

✔ In 1994, 21.2 million Americans hunted, spending over $12 billion for wildlife-related recreation.

✔ Hunting equipment such as rifles, scopes and ammunition cost hunters $3.3 billion.

✔ 10.7 million hunters hunted big game and devoted 128 million days to their sport. 3 million hunters hunted migratory waterfowl.

✔ 87% of hunters hunted only in their state of residence. 29% hunted on both public and private lands. 54% of hunters hunted only on private lands.

✔ 32% of all hunters had some college education, and 52% of the hunters earned $30,000/year or more in yearly income.

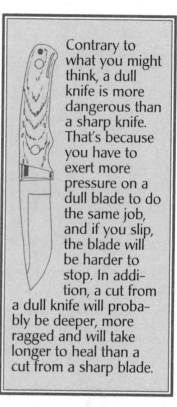

Contrary to what you might think, a dull knife is more dangerous than a sharp knife. That's because you have to exert more pressure on a dull blade to do the same job, and if you slip, the blade will be harder to stop. In addition, a cut from a dull knife will probably be deeper, more ragged and will take longer to heal than a cut from a sharp blade.

−R.STUBLER−

"Hank just can't get used to that target thrower."

Grandpa's Favorite Story

Jim Bittick, Springfield, Missouri

My grandpa loved to tell stories and this was his favorite.

Seems that when he was a young man his great passion in life was to rabbit hunt. He always found time to rabbit hunt for an hour or two every day. On weekends he would get together with a few of his friends and they would rabbit hunt most of the time. He was, however, a very God-fearing person and he always made sure to go to church every Sunday. During rabbit season he always went to the sunrise service so he would still have most of the day to hunt.

On this particular Sunday, grandpa and several of his friends arrived at church real early. They wanted to be able to get the very back seats so they could be the first ones out after the service. They were *that* dedicated to rabbit hunting. As they were waiting in their seats the pastor came to the back of the church to ring the church bell to summon the rest of his flock.

Just as he got to the belfry, the door opened and a stranger walked in. He said, "Parson, you don't know me but I would like to ask a favor of you. I have always wanted to ring a church bell and I would sure be honored if you would let me ring the bell this morning." The pastor allowed as how that would be all right and he went to the front of the church to prepare for the service.

The stranger's face lit up with a grin from ear to ear and he proceeded to climb up into the belfry tower. When he got to the bell he immediately stuck his head into the bell and began to bang his head against the inside of the bell. **Bong-bong, bong-bong,** the bell rang out across the countryside. After several minutes of this the stranger fell from the bell and landed in a dead heap at the bottom of the belfry tower.

Just then the rest of the congregation arrived at church and, horrified, they all gathered around the dead stranger. The pastor, alarmed by all the commotion, hurried to the back of the church. One of the deacons, visibly shaken, asked the pastor if he knew the stranger. The pastor answered, "I don't know his name, but his face sure rings a bell!"

The Bear That Wouldn't Die
Franklin Flack

A friend of mine named Fred was bear hunting with a friend of his a few years back. His friend was successful in taking a clean, solid broadside shot on a large bear. Knowing the bear would not go very far, and knowing he would need help in bloodtrailing and field dressing, he left to go get Fred. When the two men found the bear, they rubbed a stick against the bear's eye to verify it was dead. They then unloaded their guns and prepared for the field dressing chore. When they rolled the bear over onto its back, it let out a "woof." You can imagine how fast the two men high-tailed it out of there.

After collecting their wits (and cleaning out their shorts), they waited a half hour before returning to the bear. They slowly approached it and once again rubbed a stick against the bear's eye to verify it was dead. They laughed about the bear having one last growl left and started to roll it over for field dressing. They stopped laughing when the bear let out a second "woof." This time they didn't run away quite so far.

They sat and watched the bear for another half hour. They thought about shooting it again "just to make sure" but they noticed it hadn't moved (other than rolling back over onto its side when they ran away). They decided against shooting a second time thinking that it could not possibly still be alive. After brushing the eye to verify that the bear was dead for a third time, they decided to stick around to see what was going on. They found that every time the bear was rolled onto its back, the air trapped inside its lungs would escape, causing the "woof" sound. When the bear fell back onto its side, the lungs would once again fill up with air. Fred told me it took a while before he could sleep through the night without waking up in a cold sweat—I can only imagine his dream of having a dead bear chasing him through the woods.

Watch Your Wind

A good hunter never forgets to consider wind speed when shooting, especially on longer shots.

Here's a chart that shows bullet drift in inches at various distances and wind speeds for a 150 grain .30-06 slug (assumes 90 degree cross-wind).

	Wind Speed		
	10 mph	20 mph	30 mph
Target			
100 yds	.8 "	1.6"	2.4"
200 yds	2.9"	5.9"	9.5"
300 yds	7.6"	15.3 "	22.8"

As you can tell, wind is an important factor when taking aim at your target. No matter if you're casually plinking at 100 feet or anxiously scoping a ten-point buck at 300 yards, watch your wind!

"...so I'm guessing hunting season starts tomorrow..."

Bird Hunting

ACROSS
1. Game to practice shooting
5. Waterfowl org. (abbr.)
8. Pull the trigger
10. Wise forest bird
11. Picture
12. Two good shots
15. Mallards
19. Gun packed for travel
20. To stare at
21. _____ Eider (duck)
22. Wear during turkey season (abbr.)
24. To exist
27. Type of turkey call
28. Type of iron
29. Bunch of geese
32. Young animal
33. On a penny
34. Type of sights
36. At
37. Most you can bag
38. Some duck's head color
39. A great place to live (abbr.)
42. Small upland bird (abbr.)
43. Approval to hunt on land
45. To direct
47. Flattened circle
48. To catch, cowboy-style
49. Where the chicks are

DOWN
1. Great flushing dog
2. Pheasant
3. Great hunting club
4. Chunk of mud
6. Grouse, quail, chukar...
7. On end of bird's foot
9. Male gobblers
13. Shot material
14. Your dog is one
16. Canada goose
17. Where chicks come from
18. Used to fool ducks
23. They cut wood
24. Magnifies vision
25. Same as 17 down
26. Where birds live
28. Type of goose blind
29. Slang for woman
30. Valuable cut stone
31. Batches of puppies
35. Latin for 17 down
38. Small wading birds
40. Command to your dog
41. Like
43. Geese like this crop
44. Negative response
46. Chicago's famous track

Answers on page 187.

Wilbur Primos
President–Primos, Inc.

Pan-Fried Turkey Breast

Serves: varies. Prep Time: 10 minutes

Thin sliced strips of filleted turkey breast

Flour

Salt and pepper

Granulated garlic

Milk

Oil

Mix flour, salt, pepper and garlic to taste. Wash strips of breast in cool water and dredge in flour. Dip floured strips in milk, then flour again. Drop strips into hot oil. Fry until golden brown, turning if necessary.

Wilbur Primos grew up hunting turkeys, and was infatuated by their language. In his early hunting days, Wilbur used a box call, but realized something was missing. As he listened to more and more turkeys, he understood that turkeys were just like people; some have high voices, some low voices and some coarse voices. It was then that he decided to produce a call that would reproduce all of the sounds of the wild turkey.

Needing day–by–day contact with wild turkeys so that he could record their sounds year round, he acquired four hens and two gobblers, and affectionately named a pair Loretta and Conway. It was a real treat to Wilbur to have a wild turkey voicing her vocabulary not 18 inches from his face, and after several years of studying and recording them, he developed his first turkey call, the True Triple.

One thing led to another, and Wilbur found it too difficult to make the 500 or so calls he was making each year for friends and local sporting good stores, so he had some equipment built, making it easier to make the parts he needed for the calls.

Primos Yelpers calls are put together by hand. They stand behind their products, guaranteeing that if for any reason one of their products does not perform due to manufacturing defects, they will replace it.

Part Two

Here's the second part of our informative quiz that started on page 18. When you're ready, look on pages 66-67 for the next section of the quiz.

13) The summer coat of the whitetail is comprised of:
A. Solid hairs; B. Hollow hairs.

14) The winter coat of the whitetail is comprised of:
A. Solid hairs; B. Hollow hairs.

15) Which coat of the whitetail contains more hairs per square inch?
A. Summer coat.
B. Winter coat.
C. No difference between summer and winter coats.

16) Approximately how large is the home range of the whitetail?
A. One square mile.
B. Five square miles.
C. 10 square miles.

17) The period of rut is triggered by:
A. The first frost.
B. Photoperiodism.
C. The number of does in heat.

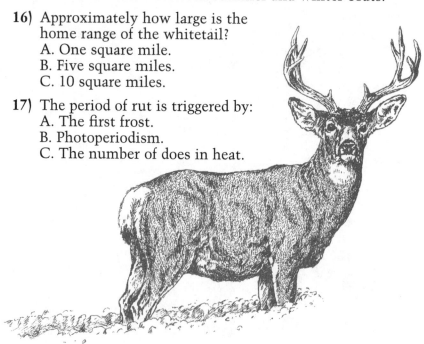

18) A "scrape" is:
   A. A small patch of ground cleared of all debris.
   B. A sapling with bark removed.
   C. A scar on polished antlers.

19) Scrapes are made:
   A. Throughout the year.
   B. While the antlers are in velvet.
   C. Only during the rut.

20) A scrape is visited and reworked:
   A. Once a day.
   B. Twice a week.
   C. Once a week.
   D. With no regular pattern.

21) After making a scrape, the buck:
   A. Always urinates in it.
   B. Never urinates in it.
   C. Sometimes urinates in it.

22) During the breeding season, white-tailed bucks:
   A. Collect does and form harems.
   B. Establish breeding territories and prevent other bucks from entering.
   C. Both of the above.
   D. Neither of the above.

23) White-tailed does come into heat:
   A. Once a year.
   B. Once every 28 days during the rut until successfully bred.
   C. Once a week during the rut.

24) A doe's heat period lasts approximately:
   A. 30 hours.
   B. One week.
   C. One month.

25) Doe fawns:
   A. Are never bred.
   B. Are sometimes bred,
   C. Are bred with the same frequency as older does.

Answers are on page 184.

Poaching Doesn't Pay

While spending time in jail for illegally taking deer, a poacher received a letter from his wife. She wrote, "Now that it's spring, I need to plant the potatoes. With you in the slammer, how am I going to dig up the backyard to do the planting?

The prisoner sent back, "I'm not sure how to solve your problem but make sure you never reveal our secret. No matter what, do not ever tell anyone about our life's savings buried in the backyard."

The next week the poacher received another letter, "A bunch of men came and dug up our backyard, they wouldn't tell me what they were looking for. What should I do?"

He wrote back, "Now plant the potatoes."

"With my coffee you won't fall asleep waitin' for a deer..."

First Buck In Camp
Bryan Carnathan

It was 3:30 a.m. when the alarm went off. I'm not sure I had slept well through all of the excitement, but I did know what day it was: opening day of the 1979 buck season.

We had left the Sunday before the opening day of buck season for a friend's house where we would be staying in Potter County, Pennsylvania. My uncle, a friend, Dad and I crammed into my uncle's four-wheel drive pickup and were on our way. Another uncle and cousin would meet us there later that night.

The first thing I noticed when the alarm went off at 3:30 a.m. was that it was pouring rain; not just drizzling or misting, it was pouring! We got dressed, checked our gear and ate a hearty breakfast. We made plans about who was standing where and who was going with whom. Dad decided he would put me on a stand where, two years ago, he had shot a buck. He would hunt in the same area and stay near me.

It was 6:00 when we headed for our stands with raincoats and insulated boots. I decided I wasn't going to let a little rain spoil my day.

Dad took me to my stand and described where he would be. We picked a place to meet for lunch, unless I got too wet or cold, and then I would go back to the truck. After Dad advised me from which direction the deer would likely come, we wished each other good luck and parted.

The woods was noisy with the driving rain hitting my raincoat and the leaves on the ground. What an ugly day. There was no snow which I had hoped for and it was raining, but at least it wasn't awful cold. The men told me the weather could be bad, but this was ridiculous. I hunched up inside my raincoat to try to keep dry.

Soon, enough light was penetrating the clouds that I could make out something white. Was it a deer's tail or another hunter? I watched, straining my eyes to make it out. Finally I saw its white neck spot and ears, along with its tail. By now my heart was going a mile a minute.

continued on page 48

47

Slowly, I raised my scoped rifle to have a better look. Then, *whack!* To my disappointment, a branch I hadn't noticed snagged on my rifle and flew back into my plastic raincoat. I could make out two tails fleeing through the woods. Was this how the rest of the day would go?

Time passed. I started to get wet and cold. I caught a glimpse of a turkey flying off its roost. Where are they during turkey season? I scouted the valley behind me, which is the grown-ups' way of saying I couldn't sit still any longer and had to move. I decided to look for Dad.

He said seven deer had walked past him, but they were all does. That warmed me up a little, so I walked around the ridge to get to an old apple orchard and I left Dad on his stand. He never seems to get cold or bored when we go hunting. I sat there awhile, thinking and watching. All I saw was a big gray squirrel who didn't seem to mind the rain. By now it was getting close to lunch time. I walked back to where Dad was sitting in the morning which was close to where we were going to meet for lunch. I couldn't find the exact spot, so I picked one near it. At least I would be in the right area. Just before I sat down, a small doe trotted past at approximately 20 yards. Now if that doesn't warm you up!

I sat down with a little more confidence. I wasn't there long before it was time to meet Dad for lunch. I stood up and it began to rain harder. By now I was soaked, to say the least. The rain had found holes in my raincoat. My coat sleeves and pants legs worked like sponges, soaking the water up to an area on me that wasn't wet yet. My fluorescent orange hunting hat had slowly lost its battle against the rain and was beginning to lose its shape. I started out for the rendezvous with Dad, but changed my mind and went back to the truck to put on dry clothes and eat lunch.

I put on one of Dad's wool shirts (I didn't mind the itch at first), my water-resistant small game hunting coat and another jacket, along with my raincoat. As I sat eating lunch in the truck, I made plans on where I would go in the afternoon. I knew that I couldn't get my deer if I kept moving around like this morning.

Eventually, after I finished eating, I worked my way back to the orchard. When I got there, the rain had stopped. "This could be a nice day yet, " I thought to myself.

I removed the lens cap from my scope and put the raincoat in my game pouch. It felt a lot better not having that cumbersome thing hanging all over me.

It was about 2:30 when I headed back to where I had seen all of the other deer. As I moved quietly to my stand, the sun even came out between the clouds. The wind was blowing hard and had dried the trees on one side, making a beautiful scene. A grouse startled me as it flushed, reminding me of the past small game season.

I finally got to the area I wanted to reach. I selected a stand between two deer trails that ran parallel to each other, about 75 yards apart. I was just about to sit down when I noticed two deer running below me. I looked for antlers but couldn't see any. As they were going out of range, I noticed the second deer was a small spike. Before I had a chance to think, five other deer had run into view along the same trail, about 50 yards away.

One deer was carrying a rack that stuck out beyond its ears. I concentrated on him and squeezed off a shot. My Remington 760 .30-06 roared, but I didn't notice the sound or recoil. I thought I had missed him, but before I knew it he was running straight for me. I got ready for a second shot, but I didn't have to use it. He spun around and fell less than 10 yards away! I hurried over, shaking and excited. The first thing I did after seeing he was dead for sure was count the points. There were four nice points to each side. I couldn't believe I had taken a

continued on page 50

First Buck In Camp
continued from page 49

running eight-point buck with one shot.

Field dressing the deer brought back pleasant memories of my first deer, one which I will always remember. I filled out the game tag and began the long drag back to the truck, reminiscing all the way.

Back at the truck, numerous people stopped to look at him. As I sat on the tailgate of the truck, drinking a Coke and eating a dry sandwich, I wondered how the other men had done. The game warden stopped to check him and then hurried on after congratulating me. When Dad got to the truck, he smiled wider than I did.

Later, back at the house, we exchanged the day's stories with the other hunters. My uncle had connected on a nice three-pointer, but everyone else had gone blank. I was king for the day.

There are many good points to getting a buck, but there are bad points too. You can't go doe hunting and Dad wouldn't let me take off school just to go along for the fun of being in the woods. One other thing, the older men who didn't get deer didn't seem as happy as before I got my big eight-pointer and they didn't talk to me much that night.

Grab A Snapshot Of Your Hunting Gear

When all your hunting gear is laid out prior to a trip, grab a quick snapshot of your equipment, It could come in handy in a number of ways.

If your gear is lost or stolen, this will help you in identifying it.

The next time you go on a similar trip, you can glance at the photo to refresh your memory on what you took last time. You'll also most likely recall what you could have done without and what you forgot to take on that trip. Finally, the shot makes an interesting addition to your hunting photo album along with shots from the hunt and you with your trophy.

Archery Word Search

```
P  R  A  D  C  T  I  D  R  A  U  G  M  R  A
C  E  O  R  E  F  F  R  T  T  E  D  S  N  U
S  E  E  A  V  Q  F  A  N  T  H  N  T  E  R
I  G  L  W  R  U  O  W  I  H  E  U  A  T  G
A  R  B  L  U  I  T  W  O  R  S  O  B  O  N
W  W  A  E  C  V  E  E  P  S  A  P  I  K  I
A  B  C  N  E  E  L  I  G  E  E  M  L  E  H
R  O  P  G  R  R  Y  G  N  O  L  O  I  U  C
D  W  R  T  B  O  W  H  I  T  E  C  Z  U  T
R  S  N  H  C  E  D  T  K  R  R  G  E  A  E
E  T  R  A  N  H  W  A  C  Q  I  W  R  T  L
V  R  M  T  S  E  R  W  O  R  R  A  E  D  F
O  I  F  S  H  A  F  T  N  N  L  L  I  M  B
O  N  P  I  R  G  Z  R  H  I  S  I  G  H  T
T  G  W  O  R  R  A  E  D  E  L  E  E  H  W
```

ARM GUARD	DRAW WEIGHT	QUIVER
ARROW	FLETCHING	RECURVE
ARROW REST	GRIP	RELEASE
BOWSTRING	LET OFF	SHAFT
CABLE	LIMB	SIGHT
CAM	NOCKING POINT	STABILIZER
COMPOUND	OVERDRAW	WHEEL
DRAW LENGTH		

Answers are on page 186.

Palace In The Popples

It's a smoky, raunchy boars' nest
　　With an unswept, drafty floor
And pillowticking curtains
　　And knife scars on the door.
The smell of a pine-knot fire
　　From a stovepipe that's come loose
Mingles sweetly with the bootgrease
　　And the Copenhagen snoose.

There are work-worn .30-30's
　　With battered, steel-shod stocks,
And drying lines of longjohns
　　And of steaming, pungent socks.
There's a table for the Bloody Four
　　And their game of two-card draw,
And there's deep and dreamless sleeping
　　On bunk ticks stuffed with straw.

Jerry and Jake stand by the stove,
  Their gun-talk loud and hot,
And Bogie has drawn a pair of kings
  And is raking in the pot.
Frank's been drafted again as cook
  And is peeling some spuds for stew
While Bruce wanders by in baggy drawers
  Reciting "Dan McGrew."

No where on earth is fire so warm
  Nor coffee so infernal,
Nor whiskers so stiff, jokes so rich,
  Nor hope blooming so eternal.
A man can live for a solid week
  In the same old underbritches
And walk like a man and spit when he wants
  And scratch himself where he itches.

I tell you, boys, there's no place else
  Where I'd rather be, come fall,
Where I eat like a bear and sing like a wolf
  And feel like I'm bull-pine tall.
In that raunchy cabin out in the bush
  In the land of the raven and loon,
With a tracking snow lying new to the ground
  At the end of the Rutting Moon.

*(The above poem was found on the wall of an abandoned deer hunting
shack in St. Louis County, Minnesota, by NAHC member Dick
Armstrong of Hoyt Lakes, who sent it along to us for publication.)*

Persistence Pays

Dan Trawicki

Without perseverence, I never would have been in the woods to take my 188-pound deer. Without persistence I never would have rattled the one final time that brought the 10-pointer in. Without persistence I never would have found the buck after I hit him.

I am here to tell fellow NAHC members persistence pays when it comes to whitetail hunting. Before I got my 10-pointer, I had vowed to try 100 percent to bag a big buck. And I had vowed I was going to do it by rattling him up.

The area I selected to hunt may seem a little unorthodox, but again persistence paid off. My hunting stand is about 15 or 20 miles from downtown Milwaukee—the largest metropolitan area in Wisconsin. It's an area that most people don't even realize is open to hunting. I knew the hunting pressure on this private property was light, and I knew some big bucks inhabited the area.

Some friends and I were hunting on a Saturday afternoon in early November. The rut was well underway, and I had been hunting every day for a couple of weeks.

I got to my stand about noon and got ready. I was using a rattling strategy which says clash the antlers together in a 15- to 20-second burst once ever hour. So once things were quieted down after climbing into my stand I rattled. That was 12:30.

I waited. Nothing happened. 1:30 rolled around. I rattled again. I waited...2:30, rattle...3:30, rattle.

It was 20 minutes after 4:00 and everything was really dead calm. The antlers produced such a loud clash I was afraid to rattle them again, but I told myself, "You said you were going to give this a try, so do it!"

I hung up my bow, picked up the horns and slammed them together for 15 seconds. I was just hanging the antlers back on their hook when I heard a deer coming. I couldn't see him yet, but I could hear him coming straight at me.

My stand was only about 150 yards from a county road. A couple of cars went by making a lot of noise, and my ears lost track of him. I knew he was in a stand of pines about 40 yards away from me, but I still couldn't see him.

After the cars passed he moved again. He popped his head out of the pines; he was still coming straight at me. He had his head down, like he was looking to find out what was making all the noise. He moved to within five yards of the base of the tree I was in and he was looking up!

I knew I couldn't draw, but I also knew he wouldn't see me if I stayed still and let my camo blend into the pine trees behind me. Everything was really quiet.

The buck began to move away and my chance came when he was 11 yards out. I drew very slowly, telling myself I had all the time in the world. *Whapp!* I hit the release and the arrow struck home.

It looked like a shoulder shot that might have gone a little far forward, but the buck went down.

In a second he was up again and bounded into the thick pines. I was using a string tracker and the line was flowing out quickly. Then it stopped.

continued on page 56

Knife Lore

There are all sorts of stories about Jim Bowie and the knife associated with his name. In reality, the famed "Bowie" knife was actually designed and first made by Jim's brother, knifemaker Rezin Bowie, in 1827, which he gave to his brother as a gift.

One of the most interesting antique knives around is the puzzle knife. These folding beauties have dials on the handle that must be turned just so in order to open the blade. The solution to the "puzzle" or combination was known only to the knife's owner so it couldn't be used against him.

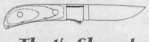

That's Sharp!

We have a friend that honed his hunting knife to such a sharp edge that when he pulled it out of the sheath, the shadow lopped two blades off his ceiling fan.

Persistence Pays *continued from page 55*

I was mad at myself because I figured I could have made a better shot at that short range. I guessed that either the arrow had pulled out or the string had broken. There was no way that shot could have killed him in such a short distance.

I waited for about 20 minutes. It was starting to get pretty dark, so I climbed out of the tree and laid the tracker spool near the trunk. I planned to follow the string on my way out of the woods. If I jumped him, the tracker line would continue to spool out. If I found that the line was broken or the arrow had pulled out, I'd come back and follow him up in the morning.

The string lead me straight down the opening between two rows of the mature planted pines which were due east of my stand. Following the string, I stopped every few steps to look and listen, just in case. About 60 yards further along I came to the end of the broken string. I found a little bit of blood on the string, but still not a drop on the ground. I considered my options. I couldn't find any blood; not a single drop, and I thought about giving up. But I thought I could see where the pine needles had been kicked up by the deer's hooves.

Since he had been running straight, I decided to continue down that row out to the dirt road. Even though I was still mad at myself for the shot and was sure I wouldn't find him, I sneaked along, stopping often, just in case.

Something caused me to glance to my left and I saw a patch of white. I walked over and there was my buck as dead as could be.

Later I determined that the arrow caught him inside the shoulder, just missing the shoulder blade. The broadhead severed the arteries in his neck and caused him to hemmorrhage, but all the bleeding was internal, just under the hide. Persistence was *everything* in finding that buck!

Table Talk

Late to arrive at hunting camp last season, a man walked into the cabin and found three of his hunting buddies sitting at the table playing poker with a dog. "Do you mean to tell me that this dog can actually read cards?" he asked.

"He sure can, but he ain't much of a poker player," replied one of his friends. "Whenever he gets a good hand, he wags his tail."

"...Nobody said, 'Hey Al, hunting season starts today,"
...you must be hearing things."

Loony Laws
Robert Pelton

No hunting rabbits from a motor boat? Illegal to shoot game birds from a trolley? Absolutely no hunting on your wedding day? Legal to carry a gun only when pursued by wild Indians? A wife legally able to hide and bury your old hunting clothing? Against the law to shoot buffalo from the windows of the barracks?

John Florio, way back in 1578, described how he felt laws were made: "The law groweth of sin, and doth punish it!" If this is truly the case, then how would anyone determine what kind of sin must have taken place for the following old laws to have been thought up and passed? Some old ignored laws sound silly when read out of context, but others are just plain ridiculous all the time.

You can't hunt while riding a camel in Harrisburg, Pennsylvania.

For example, in Knoxville, Tennessee, an ordinance states that it's illegal for anyone to shoot a jackrabbit or a hare while riding a trolley within the city limits. And Idaho retains an old piece of legislation which outlaws the hunting of game birds from their "interurban trolley system." To do so brings a $500 fine and six months in jail.

Going on an extended hunting trip in the wilderness? Don't plan on bathing if you happen to be in Rayle, Georgia. A special law prohibits hunters from taking a bath "in any lake, river or stream," while engaging in a hunt.

It's strictly against the law to go hunting on your wedding day in Victoria, Mississippi. No man can legally leave his new bride alone and go hunting with the boys on this special day. The penalty? "Imprisonment in the county jail for not more than one (1) month or by a fine of $100, or by both fine and imprisonment."

A prospective groom must "prove" his manhood before he will be allowed to marry his best girl in quiet little Truro, Massachusetts. How can a man accomplish such a feat? Easy! All the beau must do is go hunting and shoot either six blackbirds or three crows. These must be presented to his prospective father-in-law for approval.

Kansas retains an odd old law which prohibits hunters from shooting rabbits while riding around in a motor boat! And Washington bans duck hunting from a rowboat "unless the huntsman is always visible from the waist up."

You aren't allowed to hunt squirrels from a motorcycle in Tangier, Virginia.

If you happen to be in Ohio, and married, you may have some problems with your wife. According to the law, a wife is entitled to at any time burn hubby's old hunting clothes. All she must do is to "feel the need." And the husband can't do a thing about her actions!

In Fort Warren, Wyoming, it's still against the law to lean out of a barracks window and take pot shots at roving buffalo! And the parade grounds at Fort Huachuca, Arizona, are off limits to buffalo hunters! No one is allowed to shoot one of these creatures while standing during a parade or a military inspection.

But Kinsman, Arizona, tops them all! No camels can be hunted within the city limits. Nor can you hunt elephants in Pleasantville, Iowa. And you can hunt grizzly bears in Alaska, but you aren't allowed "to disturb a grizzly bear in order to take its picture."

No skunk hunting in Minneapolis, Minnesota? A hunter isn't even allowed "to tease or torment skunks" according to the city ordinance. And the legislature in Pennsylvania even passed a special law against hunters which they called the "Act for the Better Protection of Skunks."

Were you even aware that clay pigeons are bred in the state of Kentucky? They passed a strange law which declares that it's illegal "to shoot clay pigeons during the breeding season." And in North Dakota, an old law prohibits hunters from going to sleep while wearing boots.

continued on page 60

Michigan is a true friend of all duck hunters! This state doesn't allow anyone to "scare" wild ducks that someone else is about to shoot. Anyone frightening such ducks will be fined severely and jailed!

No hunting frogs on a Sunday in Little Mullen, Nebraska.

Some areas of the country have a multitude of Sunday hunting and gun regulations. For example, in Wichita, Kansas, citizens aren't allowed to hunt on the Sabbath with a slingshot. You can forget your dreams of hunting on the Sabbath in Fayetteville, Arkansas. A city ordinance forbids even the shooting of a cockroach. The law states that it's "illegal to kill any living creature" on a Sunday.

Going to visit friends in South Carolina? Be sure and take along your gun if you plan on attending church. An old law declares that "every law abiding citizen" must carry a gun to church. And according to this same law, he is not "obliged to leave his gun" outside upon entering the church.

You can't go hunting on Sunday in Indiana unless you happen to be under the age of 14. And in North Carolina, hunting on the Sabbath is banned unless a dog accompanies the hunter.

But this old Vermont law beats them all! It was obviously designed to protect their women. No married female is allowed on the streets on the Sabbath unless she is properly protected. How? Her husband is required by law to carry his "musket" and walk within 20 steps behind her at all times.

Many gun laws are rather ridiculous. For example, the state of Oklahoma technically wasn't the greatest place for hunters! An old statute says that no person can legally carry a gun unless he is being pursued by "wild Indians."

All "space guns" are outlawed in North Andover, Massachusetts. A strict city ordinance doesn't allow anyone to "own, carry or use" any type of "space gun."

Lost your can opener and out in the wilds on a hunt? Getting desperate for some food? If so, you can shoot open that can of beans in Spades, Indiana. But be sure and do this with your rifle. This community has an odd law which prohibits anyone from opening a can of food by shooting at it with a revolver!

It's a "gross misdemeanor" in Onalaska, Washington, for any adult to give a "toy pistol" to any child under the age of 18. All gun owners within the city limits of Albuquerque, New Mexico, must check in "all shooting irons" with the chief of police. This must be done within one half hour of entering the community.

Dueling with water pistols is actually outlawed throughout the state of Massachusetts. And in Louisiana, you can't shoot at a bank teller with a water pistol!

Norfolk County, Virginia, has an odd law regulating how a person may hunt. No one can use a rifle for hunting unless they are "at least 15 feet up off the ground." And in Connecticut it's actually against the law to chew tobacco while carrying a gun, unless, that is, the person has the permission of a doctor— and this had better be in writing!

It's against the law in Kansas to hunt ducks with a mule.

These areas are certainly not recommended for anyone who enjoys hunting! Take Missouri, for example. This state prohibits all uncaged bears from walking on their highways. All wild animals in Lubbock, Texas, must be kept on a strong leash. No lions or tigers are allowed to "roam the city streets" of Alderson, West Virginia. And in Rock Springs, Montana, no wild animals, specifically bears, are allowed "to run at will" in the town. Lastly, tigers, lions, bears, wildcats, panthers and orangutans are banned from the city limits of Nachusa, Illinois.

"We bury men when they are dead, but we try to embalm the dead body of laws, keeping the corpse in sight long after the vitality has gone," declared Henry Ward Beecher. It seems from all of the above that he was not far off track. Most of these laws were passed many years ago and have been forgotten with the passage of time.

Beecher concluded: "It usually takes a hundred years to make a law; and then, after it has done its work, it usually takes another hundred years to get rid of it."

*The author wrote the book **LOONY LAWS**, published by Walker and Company, New York. Reprinted from **North American Hunter**.*

Theorems Applying To Wild Game Cookery

No new recipe is ever a total failure; it can always serve as a bad example.

Culinary expertise is inversely proportional to kitchens ruined and meals burned.

If anything can go wrong, check the oven because it may have already.

WHEN YOU RETURN FROM THE STORE AND BEGIN TO PREPARE A WILD GAME RECIPE, THERE WILL ALWAYS BE ONE INGREDIENT YOU FORGOT TO BUY.

According to your hunting buddies, there is always an ingredient which, when added to or subtracted from your recipe, will provide a better tasting meal.

He who complains about the camp cook's meals becomes the new cook.

If the recipe works perfectly this time, you won't be able to remember what you did right for next time.

Having the butcher drop meat into the bag you are holding does not justify telling your dinner guests that you "bagged" this meal.

When all else fails, re-read the recipe.

When re-reading the recipe fails, blame it on a printing error.

"...You're not that good of a shot...why do you hunt boar?"

There's these two best friends deer hunting. One says to the other, "You go that way and I'll go this way." One hour goes by. Moe sees some brush moving so he takes aim and without thinking he unloads on the brush. He goes over to see what he's shot and it's his friend Joe. Moe says "Oh my God, what have I done?!" So he takes Joe to the hospital.

Two hours go by. The doctor walks out and says, "I'm sorry but your friend didn't make it. It was pretty bad in there." Moe says, "I didn't mean to do it."

"Well," the doctor says. "He would've had a chance if you didn't field dress him."

–Life Member Michael Vitiello, Fort Lauderdale FL

I Held The Antler Of My First Deer – Before I Shot Him

John Davis, Natchitoches, Louisiana

I love to hunt. So much, that I'd try giving up eating rather than hunting, if it came to pickin' and choosin'.

I bagged a whole bunch of squirrels and rabbits. But, even though I'm 22, and have hunted deer many times, I was never able to kill me a deer — until 1978.

Now me getting my first deer is no big deal to ya'll. But a certain thing happened about the deer I killed that might not happen again in a lifetime of hunting.

One morning, about the first of November, my hunting buddies and I decided to go hunting at Tar Branch Bottom, a place near where Carter, one of my friends, lives. My friends are Carter, Delbert and Sidney Moore from Spanish Lake Community, near Robeline, Louisiana.

Well, before we went hunting, we were hashing over different things, like who's done killed a deer this season and who hasn't. Carter volunteered he hadn't killed one, but that yesterday he was hunting at Tar Branch and found the left horn of what looked to be a six point buck. It was bloody on the end. So we figured the deer must have gotten in a fight with another buck or something, and that the horn got broken off.

Anyway, we headed off for the woods, and everybody took their stands. I had my .30-30 ready and waiting. About three hours passed, and I said to myself that in about two more hours I would probably go home.

About that time, I heard the limbs breaking and the

leaves crunching—and there he was! He stopped about forty feet from my stand. And then I laid him down. My shot hit him between the shoulder and the neck, and he fell in his tracks. My friends heard the shot, so they came on over.

We examined the size and all, and then noticed the buck had only one horn. The left horn had been broken off. We hurried up and field dressed him and came back to Carter's house to see if by any chance the horn that Carter had found the day before was the horn of my deer. We placed the horn in the appropriate position and it fit perfectly. The horn also had a sliver-like piece on the end where it had been broken off, and it fit the form of the broken piece in the head of the deer. The match was confirmed.

Now, who would ever think that I was looking at and holding the horn of the deer in the morning that I was gonna kill later that day. He was a 6-pointer and field dressed about 125 pounds. I'm waiting for the head to be mounted. That's one deer I'll never forget.

·THE GREAT· Whitetail Quiz

Part Three

Here's the third part of our informative quiz that started on page 18. When you're ready, look on pages 78-79 for more quiz questions.

26) Normally whitetails produce:
   A. A surplus of young each year.
   B. Enough fawns to replace those deer that die of old age.
   C. Always one fawn per doe.
   D. Always two fawns per doe.

27) Carrying capacity is defined as:
   A. The fall production of a deer herd.
   B. The ability of a given area of land to support a given number of a given species at a given time without harming the habitat for future populations.
   C. The number of animals the land can support during the summer months.

28) The best way to increase the carrying capacity for a long period of time is to:
   A. Improve the habitat.
   B. Conduct artificial feeding programs.
   C. Harvest only bucks.

29) One of the earliest attempts to control the size of deer populations was to:
   A. Establish bag limits and closed seasons.
   B. Regulate hunter numbers.
   C. Prohibit shooting of does.

30) The best way to maintain a deer population near the carrying capacity is to:
   A. Harvest bucks only.
   B. Harvest bucks and some does.
   C. Implement artificial feeding programs.
   D. Prohibit hunting until the deer population exceeds the carrying capacity.

31) Nationwide, the most significant deer predator, excluding man, is the:
A. Wolf.
B. Cougar.
C. Domestic dog.

32) Eliminating all predators from deer range usually results in:
A. A long-term increase in the deer population.
B. Habitat destruction by deer due to overbrowsing as deer numbers increase beyond the carrying capacity.
C. An early rut.

33) In general, the most serious problem confronting whitetails today is:
A. Overharvest by hunters.
B. Poaching.
C. Habitat loss.

34) Winter severity becomes critical for whitetails when:
A. Snow depths exceed eight inches and temperature drops below the freezing point.
B. There is a 30-day period with more than 18 inches of snow cover and below average temperatures.
C. There is a 30-day period with 12 or more inches of snow cover and the temperatures fall below 30 degrees.

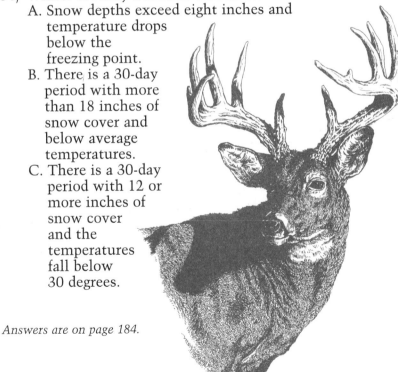

Answers are on page 184.

Know Your Knives!

Draw a line to the knife that matches the style of blade.

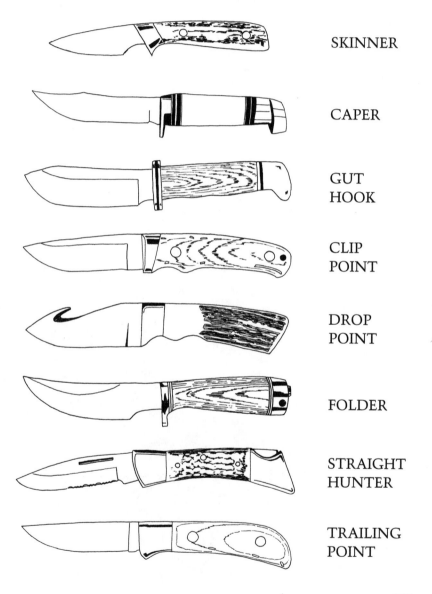

SKINNER

CAPER

GUT
HOOK

CLIP
POINT

DROP
POINT

FOLDER

STRAIGHT
HUNTER

TRAILING
POINT

Answers are on page 189.

The Elk With The Lady's Name On It

By. L. C. Trimber, as told to Brook Elliott

Years ago, I guided for an outfitter in Idaho. We had just finished packing about 150 bales of hay into our early season camp, when George the outfitter, said to me, "LC, I've got this man, and I'd like you to take his wife hunting. They're both very experienced sportspeople. In fact, they just came back from a 21-day African safari."

Now when old George would start trying to sell you on hunters you hadn't even met yet, a young guide like me had cause for concern. I was a bit more than apprehensive.

George was the boss and he certainly could tell me what to do, but his soft-soap continued. He went on to tell me that this fine filly was so good looking she could stand in for Marilyn Monroe in Bus Stop.

Despite my leeriness of George's approach, I said to myself, this has got to be a pretty sharp gal, right? I mean, good looking and an accomplished hunter to boot?! Who better than me to lead her to a trophy elk? Right?

I told George I'd be happy to take 'em. Then the clients showed up. My Marilyn Monroe double was in tough shape. Really tough shape. I mean this gal was two mules wide and about 12 hands high. Must have gone 240 on the hoof, standing about five feet, three inches. She was blonde, I'll give her that, but that was the only similarity to Marilyn.

Their first night in camp, I talked the couple through the various procedures for the hunt. I stressed that we would use the horses instead of just walking. This gal was all for that, although I had my doubts about her ability to even get on a horse, let alone keep it under control.

"One thing," she said to me. "I don't care how big a bull we get, as long as it's bigger than my husband's!"

Her husband, Jack, had killed his only bull the year before, and it scored about 180 at the most, so I didn't think there

continued on page 70

would be a problem. We'd get us a small 3x4, or something like that, and she would be happy. Little did I know.

Next morning we were up for breakfast at 4:30, and I started packing the horses. She said she'd fix lunches and get ready. Then she disappeared for about half an hour.

When she emerged from her tent, she was ready alright! She had put on all her makeup. I mean she wore this heavy duty stuff—powder, rouge, lipstick and who knows what all. And she had on her hunting outfit. Looked like she had come right out of Eddie Bauer. Had those britches on with the extra seat sewed in the back, for instance. And had on her riding boots, real fancy jobs. I thought she had a pair of hunting boots as well, but all she'd brought were these west Texas roach killers.

We took off on the horses and got into the country I wanted to hunt. Picketing the horses, we moved down maybe 150 yards. She wasn't going any farther. Just couldn't make it.

It was just breaking daylight and in this country, right when the sun comes up, it turns cold real quick. So, naturally, I had to build her a fire.

And there we were, sitting under this tree with this fire going, right when we should have been out hunting.

Things weren't looking good. I told her we would have to get into some other country if we were going to get an elk. She said, "Fine. Why don't you get the horses and I'll wait here."

I was less than 50 yards away when she decided that being alone wasn't going to work for her. She started squealing and hollering for me to come back, not to leave her. She was scared to be alone!

So that took care of day one. We went back to camp, and spent the rest of the day drinking coffee, telling hunting stories and stuff. Had a grand old time of it, too.

The next day we went through the same process. I figured if I could keep her on horseback, we would be a whole lot better off. We even left a little later in the morning because she said she was so cold. So it was well after daylight when we actually got started.

We were pausing in some boulders, out of the wind, when she tells me again how important it is to get an elk bigger than Jack's. And just then I heard an elk busting through the brush, coming from the north side of the ridge.

I told her not to get excited, everything would be fine, but to get ready because an elk was coming through the woods. And there he came, a 6x6 bull that would score 360 easy.

So here's this experienced African hunter, with all those animals to her credit. And at 40 yards she put the crosshairs on his chest, pulled the trigger, and missed! That bullet went clear over his back.

But the bull didn't bolt! Instead, he turned down the hill and ambled off. Now maybe he was 60 yards out, and she threw the gun up again, pulled the trigger and missed again. This time she fired in front of him.

I told her to relax, and squeeze off the shot. Everything would be fine. She tossed that custom-built Mauser to her shoulder once more, sighted through that expensive scope once more, and fired once more, just as the bull turned

continued on page 72

around a point of rocks and went out of sight. There was a crashing sound as he went down!

Before I could say anything she ran down to those rocks. And there was that bull, a whole lot bigger than Jack's, laying on the ground.

Before I could stop her, she was down there, and had her tag slapped on the bull. She was all excited, jumping up and down, and couldn't wait to get some pictures. I was afraid she was going to have a heart attack or something, and I spent some time just calming her down. I got so busy with her, I didn't think to check for bullet holes, blood or anything.

She finally relaxed a bit and repaired her make-up (she carried a whole kit of the stuff in a saddle bag), and we got ready to take pictures,

I decided the angle was wrong, and lifted the bull's rack to move him. Just then he decided to wake up and make tracks elsewhere. Now, I rodeoed a lot when I was younger, and have grabbed ahold of horns before, but never like this!

The bull was shaking his head, while I hung on for dear life. She was yelling, "Hold him! Hold him, LC!" Meanwhile, I was yelling, "Don't shoot! Please, don't shoot!"

This went on for maybe a couple minutes, but it felt like five years. Finally, I let go where I could roll in a snowbank, out of the bull's way and he continued down the hill.

I had barely caught my breath, when we heard shots about a half mile off in the direction the bull had taken. Mounting up, we rode down there. Sure enough, there was our bull on the ground, with these boys just about finished field dressing him.

Now the fun really started. She had seen this bull fall in front of her rifle, and it was certainly bigger than Jack's. And she was not going through all of this again if she could help it.

"Thanks for stopping my elk," she told them fellers.

"Do what?" was the natural reply.

"I said, thanks for stopping my elk. I shot him up on the hill and he's mine."

Well these boys weren't buying any of that. They shot him. They knew they shot him. That was final, and they let her know it in no uncertain terms.

Finally she said, "I don't want to argue about it. That's my elk and that's all there is to it."

So one of them said, kind of sarcastic-like, "Waddaya mean your elk? You got your name on it?"

"As a matter of fact, I do," she replied. "Here, I'll show you."

You can imagine their reaction when she showed them her tag already attached. And, of course, the elk belonged to whoever tagged it.

But things worked out for those boys, too. For them, elk was really a side thing. They were from back East, and had come out for mule deer. So I told them I would be back the next day, and put them onto some mulies to make up for their trouble.

Everybody wound up happy.

"Dear, remember when you said for your birthday you wanted a new pump?"

Just A Bump On The Head?

Donald Speiser

Black bear like swamps, so that's where my brother-in-law and hunting partner Frank Fairchild and I set our baits. It didn't matter that the area we were hunting didn't have any trees tall enough for us to place our tree-stands because we like to hunt from ground blinds. That way, we are on the same level as the bears.

I was hunting with my .50 Hawkins black powder rifle. I also carried my Ruger Super Blackhawk .44 Magnum on my hip, just in case I had to finish a bear off. The Hawkins shoots extremely well, so I wasn't worried about anything. It's just slow to load. The .44 is a lot more convenient.

It was around 3:00 in the afternoon on the third day of the Minnesota bear season when we got to our stands. About 45 minutes later I heard something moving to my left. My pulse quickened when I turned and spotted a huge black bear feeding on the bait pile 12 yards away. I turned slowly, raised the Hawkins and fired at the bear's head, the only target I had.

When the white smoke cleared, the bear lay before me.

Frank, who was hunting near me, came over after the shot to help me gut the animal. We were just going to roll the bear over when it grunted a couple times. Frank said, "Don, I think you'd better finish him off, he's coming back to life," so I shot him again, this time with the .44 Magnum.

Later, when we were skinning the bear out, we were shocked to find only one bullet hole in him—and that was from the .44 Mag. We looked, but we couldn't find the Hawkins ball. Finally, we noticed a small furrow on the bear's scalp. The round ball had bounced off his head!

I made a rug of the bear's hide and it now hangs in my living room with my other trophies. I still shudder to think what could have happened if I didn't have the .44 along and the bear came to before I could reload my Hawkins. A 417-pound Minnesota black bear with a headache can do a lot of damage!

As the schoolbus approached Johnny's house one morning, the driver noticed that Johnny was propped up against a tree next to the driveway...sound asleep! So he gave the horn a little toot to wake him.

As Johnny got on the bus, the driver asked why he was so tired this morning. "You're usually just full of energy," the driver said.

So Johnny told him the story: "I had a very long night, sir. Yesterday evening, me and Pa went fishing and caught us each a stringer full of catfish, so we stayed up pretty late cleaning them.

We finally got to bed and at about one in the morning we got woke up by a loud commotion out in the henhouse. Pa said, "I'm finally going to catch that fox in the act!" So he loaded up his trusty side-by-side, I grabbed a flashlight and we sneaked out the back door in our nightgowns and slippers.

We got up to the henhouse and the fox was still raising Cain with the chickens, so I slowly opened the door and aimed the flashlight in as Pa cocked his shotgun and poked it through.

Just then our old bloodhound, Sam, reached up under Pa's nightgown and cold-nosed him.

Man, oh, man!! We was up all night, cleaning chickens."

★ ★ ★ ★ ★ ★ ★ ★ ★ ★ ★ ★

Miss an Easy Shot?

Here are some excuses that might help:

I forgot to take the safety off.

I exhaled and fogged up my scope.

The deer was too close.

The deer was too far away.

My scope must be off.

There was a tree in the way.

A gust of wind came up.

The deer jumped just when I shot.

My trigger finger was half froze.

I forgot to put a shell in the chamber.

Must have been a "dud" shell.

All I could see was hair.

I need new glasses.

I just got new glasses.

I never did like this gun.

75

Name That Track

Test your woodsman knowledge. Can you name each of the "critters" that made the following tracks?

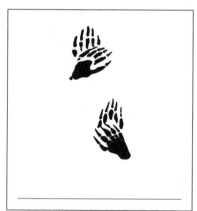

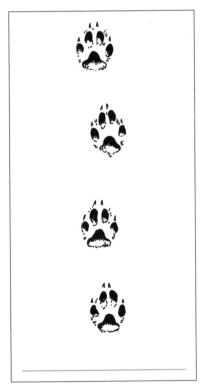

Answers are on page 190.

·THE GREAT· Whitetail Quiz

Part Four

Ready for the fourth part of our informative quiz that started on page 18? Here it is! And when you're done with these questions, you'll find more on pages 110-111.

35) A sign that deer are running short of food in the winter is:
A. Movement of deer to deer yards.
B. Bucks shed their antlers.
C. Deer eat "stuffing foods" such as balsam.

36) Periodic significant starvation during the winter indicates:
A. The deer population has exceeded the carrying capacity.
B. Artificial feeding programs should be inaugurated or increased.
C. Too many does are being shot, leaving the fawns helpless in winter.

37) When nutritional food supplies in a deer yard are exhausted:
A. Deer starve to death.
B. Deer leave the yard to look for food elsewhere.

38) The whitetail's most finely developed sense is:
A. Sight.
B. Hearing.
C. Smell.

39) The dominant animal within a group of deer is usually:
A. An adult buck.
B. An adult doe.
C. A yearling.

40) Only the bucks have a white throat patch.
A. True; B. False.

41) Only the bucks "snort."
A. True; B. False.

42) When wounded, a deer:
   A. Always flinches noticeably.
   B. Runs with its tail tucked between its legs.
   C. Both of the above.
   D. Neither of the above.

43) The buck-to-doe ratio among fawns approximates:
   A. One buck to one doe.
   B. Two bucks to one doe.
   C. Two does to one buck.

44) The most popular hunting method is:
   A. Stand hunting.
   B. Still hunting.
   C. Deer drives.

45) Rattling up bucks is most effective:
   A. As soon as bucks remove antler velvet.
   B. During the peak of the rut.
   C. Shortly before antlers are shed.

46) Stand hunting is most effective:
   A. When deer are active.
   B. During periods of high hunting pressure.
   C. When food supplies are abundant.

47) "Sign" left by wounded deer at the site of the hit almost always includes:
   A. Blood.
   B. Bone fragments.
   C. Hair.

48) Effective deer drives require:
   A. As few as two hunters.
   B. Two to six hunters.
   C. More than six hunters.

49) The best advantage offered by a tree stand versus a ground stand is:
   A. Deer never look up.
   B. Great visibility for the hunter.
   C. Deer cannot detect the scent of a tree stand hunter.

50) Most deer harvested by bow hunters are shot at a distance of:
   A. Approximately 20 yards.
   B. Approximately 40 yards.
   C. Greater than 40 yards.

Answers are on page 184.

Hunter's All-Day Pocket Biscuit

For breakfast, lunch or trail snacks, these
tasty nutritious biscuits can't be beat.

⅔ cup water
¼ cup margarine, melted
2¼ cups complete pancake mix
   (buttermilk or plain)
1 cup rolled oats, uncooked
¼ cup sugar
½ tsp. cinnamon
½ cup chopped walnuts or pecans
½ cup raisins

Thoroughly mix all dry ingredients. Add margarine and
water, mixing until dry ingredients are moistened. Drop
heaping tablespoonfuls onto greased cookie sheet. Bake 12
to 14 minutes or until light golden brown in oven preheated
to 425 degrees. Makes about a dozen delicious biscuits.

Lloyd Barnhart, West Sand Lake, New York

Painted Push Pins

Push pins painted
with a reflective
coating work well in
marking the trail to
your stand. They are
less likely to be
noticed by other
bowhunters, and
when you're entering
or leaving in low
light they will show
up extremely well in
a flashlight beam.

— RSTUBLER —

**"You better work some more
on that deer grunt, Bill."**

Amazing Big Bear Stories

Almost everyone who guides or outfits hunters for these big bear has had some close calls. Guy Anttila of Taku Safari, Inc., a guiding service in British Columbia, told me the most aggressive behavior he had ever seen displayed by a grizzly occurred in October, 1986. He and his wife were photographing grizzlies that were trying to catch salmon on the Taku River. The Anttilas had just completed their fall hunting season and were taking a break by filming bear.

It was their second day of filming, and they had recorded some good footage of several grizzlies. Now they were concentrating their efforts on a sow with a three-year-old cub still traveling with her. After an hour of chasing and eating salmon, the sow and cub crossed over to the side of the river where the Anttilas were hidden in some driftwood. Unaware of the humans' presence, the sow and cub walked into the willows and alders some 80 yards away. The Anttilas knew the sow would soon pick up their scent, as the wind was blowing toward her.

Guy assumed the sow and cub would leave the area once they picked up their scent. With their rifle leaning against the drift logs, the Anttilas discussed their photography. That's when things got interesting. Luckily, Guy was facing the right direction to see the big sow break out of the willows at a distance of 45 yards. She was coming on the run, up the scent trail, her head down in a silent charge. Sand was flying behind every step.

Anttila shouted at the bear as he reached for the rifle, but

continued on page 82

this just gave the bear a better fix on their location. The next thing Anttila knew, the open sights on his .375 H&H Magnum were centered on the bear. He instinctively shifted the aim slightly to the right to miss the face as he fired.

The bullet hit the sow in the left shoulder, stopping her.

The charge lasted only about four seconds. The sow tried to get up, but her left leg kept buckling under her. This infuriated the bear, now roaring and making all the sounds of a charging bear. A second shot through the shoulder killed her.

A similar charge happened to a guide in British Columbia, North American Hunting Club Life Member Igor Steciw. In 1979 he was guiding a hunter for moose and black bear. It was October, and the day had been cloudy with intermittent rain. Late in the afternoon, the weather cleared and Steciw thought it would be a good time to sit on a hillside and do some glassing. They were near a small, unnamed lake at the upper drainage of the Skeena River, and the coho salmon were at the height of their spawning run.

After only 15 minutes on the hillside, the two men heard the loud crack of a branch breaking, then another. When they looked toward the sound, they saw a large grizzly walking the shoreline of the lake about 300 yards away. Since the hunter didn't have a grizzly tag, they took pictures of the bear as he ambled in their direction. In the last frame Steciw took, the bear was about 25 yards away and heard the camera shutter click. That got the bear excited. It barked a few times and stood on its hind legs. Steciw called out to the bear, "Go on home, boy," expecting it to take off in a run. But the bear grunted, went back down on all fours, and stood up again.

Again Igor yelled, "Go on, get out of here." To the two men's amazement, the bear now went down on all fours and charged at full speed, taking big leaps toward the hunters. Steciw's rifle went up to his shoulder in a flash, and he fired once, twice and a third time. The third shot

turned back the charge.
The bear was now
sideways at about
20 feet. At this
point, Steciw
took aim behind
the left shoulder
and fired. The bear
wavered through
a few steps, went
down and
rolled off the
hill. All was quiet again. The bear squared 7 feet 11 inches
and was dark brown with silver tips from its forehead to
the tail.

The unpredictable nature of large bear keeps a hunter
on his toes all the time, whether he is in the field
hunting or in camp resting. A good example of this
was related to me by Jerome Knap of Canada North
Outfitting, a polar bear guiding service. One of Jerome's
hunters and an Eskimo guide were polar bear hunting at
the northern end of Baffin Island at the mouth of
Admiralty Inlet. During the first two days of the hunt, the
hunter saw nine bear, including two males in the nine-foot
class. Hunters don't normally pass up nine-foot bear, but in
this case, the hunter did so because he and his guides had
found some day-old tracks of a bear that would go over 11
feet. They decided to hold out for that bear.

On the third morning, the hunters were still asleep in an
igloo when the chained dogs started to bark. One of the
guides, thinking another dog team was approaching,
crawled out of the igloo to see what was happening. There,
just 15 yards from the igloo, was a nine-foot polar bear eating
on a seal carcass that had been shot the day before for food.
The guide retreated into the igloo and told the hunter.

Thinking it a good opportunity to photograph a polar
bear, the hunter used his knife to chip a hole in the side of
the igloo large enough to stick his camera lens through. As
he started to take a picture, the bear looked up and saw the

continued on page 84

Amazing Big Bear Stories continued from page 83

black spot on the side of the igloo. It charged instantly.

The igloo half collapsed under the bear's attack. Then, backing away, the bear spotted the men. As the bruin charged again, the hunter grabbed his rifle and shot, killing the bear two paces away.

While the brown and grizzly bear seem to dislike the scent of man, there are occasions when it doesn't seem to matter. One fall I was hunting caribou on the Alaskan Peninsula in an area of low-rolling tundra hills scattered with small lakes. There was little vegetation in the area, and long stalks were required to get near the caribou bulls found moving through the area. Walking across the wet tussocks was tough and time-consuming.

Early one morning, I spotted two large bulls about three miles from my small spike camp and set out to try for the larger of the two. By the time I got to where the bulls had been, they had moved on, putting too much distance between us to cover that day. Disappointed, I started the long walk back to camp.

As I topped the first hill on my return trip, I looked back to see a large brown bear following me some 400 yards back. He was a beautiful animal with long hair waving in the stiff breeze which blew from me to him. I didn't have a bear tag, so I just sat down to admire him and see what his plans were.

With the wind blowing toward him, he must have scented me, but it didn't seem to have any effect. When I sat down, he lay down. I waited and he waited. When I got up, he got up. Once again I headed back toward camp, now looking back more than ahead. When I would go down into a low area and couldn't see him, I would always be ready as I approached the top of the next hill, half expecting him to be in front of me.

However, he never closed the distance, and he basically did whatever I did. When I reached camp, he disappeared just as quickly as he had appeared, and I never saw him again. Not because I wasn't looking, though.

Most big bear are naturally shy, and if given the chance, would prefer to avoid a confrontation with man. But the polar bear doesn't see it that way. In fact, he has the reputation of being the only animal in the world that will instinctively stalk and kill a man. Jerome Knap points out that a polar bear doesn't have to be wounded to be dangerous, nor does it have to be disturbed or angered or have its young threatened. All you have to do is be in its kingdom of ice and snow. You are flesh, blood and bones, and thereby edible.

True Story!

In Anchorage, Alaska, a moose dropped dead on Robert Krall's front lawn, but when he called the State Department of Fish and Game to take it away, they said that they were not responsible. Municipal authorities also disclaimed any responsibility for removing the carcass. Krall tried to give the dead animal to a dog breeder, but found that it's illegal to feed moose meat to dogs. The Anchorage Zoo didn't have enough staff to send anyone for the body, and the municipal dump refused to accept it because they didn't have the equipment to bury it.

Krall finally found a dump that would accept the animal and the State Land Department sent a truck to help him out, but the brakes on the truck failed and it plunged 15 feet down a bank and buried itself in garbage. He finally paid a car-wrecker $25 to haul the dead moose away.

85

Don't Be Over-Anxious

Steve Binning

NAHC Member's Story

I was sitting on a tree that had fallen into a fork of another tree and it looked like a good spot to be in on that morning. I climbed about half way up the fallen tree and sat down. I began to rattle my antlers and it wasn't long before I saw movement. I saw a buck that looked like a good six point from where I was sitting. The buck was walking broad side coming in my direction. I said to myself that this is a perfect shot, and it was. I released the arrow and watched it hit a vital spot; the deer jumped straight up in the air and started to run.

I knew he was hit good and wouldn't go to far if I didn't chase him. I sat on the tree for about fifteen or twenty minutes and climbed down. I saw where the deer went down and started walking toward the area, then right in front of me I saw this buck take off running, I was really mad at myself because I thought that I didn't wait long enough and the buck that I shot had gotten up and started running.

I walked down to the spot where the buck I shot went down, and sure enough there laid the buck I shot dead.

What had happened was that I rattled in two bucks, each coming from opposite directions toward each other. If I wouldn't have been over anxious I could have witnessed a rare sight of two bucks fighting and the chance to have picked which buck I wanted.

I settled for the seven-point buck instead of the eight-point buck, but I was still happy regardless of the outcome of being over-anxious.

My Own Knife Almost Took My Life

NAHC Member's Story

Steve Schaust

President's Trophy Winner

For years I have been a member of the North American Hunting Club and a bunch of other organizations, so I've been reading about big game hunts for a long time. But I really got the itch to make the dream come true a few years ago. This past year the dream became a reality, but the reality was more of a nightmare.

Of all the places I wanted to hunt, Alaska held the most intrigue. Beautiful caribou, enormous moose, magnificent dall rams, splendid mountain goats, fierce bears and many more game animals than I have adjectives to describe. The only problem was that a guided hunt cost more than my salary as a Minneapolis x-ray technologist could handle.

I knew I would have to cut corners somewhere, but the problem was "How?" Over the course of two years of planning and research for this dream hunt, I discovered plenty of ways to cut the costs and still enjoy a quality hunt. The biggest dollar saving, which means a big expense in time and taking a chance, was to plan the hunt entirely on my own, without a guide. Being young and in fairly good shape helped, and so did my past experience of solo hunting in the Lower 48, even though I realize it's best to have a hunting partner.

But in Alaska, you can't hunt dall sheep or brown and grizzly bear without a guide. This still left me with many options, and my number one priority was a good-size caribou. After that, I wanted a moose, a mountain goat, and possibly a black bear. As long as this was to be a dream hunt, other possibilities I listed were black-tailed deer and other game offered on special permit hunts.

With all this in mind, I planned to go where the Boone and Crockett record book said most caribou trophies came from in Alaska—the Alaskan Peninsula—but I had to catch the migration.

I left some details open-ended to allow for sidetrips for other game if I was successful with my top priority trophies. Central and southwestern Alaska seemed good for big moose, and isolated areas along the southern coast, plus the southeaster panhandle both looked good for big mountain goats. So I made sure I had information from the Alaska Fish & Game Department, and I based my tentative side-trips on good trophy areas that were also accessible for a do-it-yourselfer like myself.

The easy part was packing up the gear, including a Remington 700 BDL 30-06 and a "bear backup" 870 Wingmaster 20 gauge, which could also feed me daily if I could hit ptarmigan or more delectable small game. The Bushnell Trophy spotting scope, a 16x36-power model, was as valuable as the hip boots I wore during 95 percent of the hunt.

The tough part was juggling my schedule, swapping days and taking vacation to come up with a total of two months away from work. When that fell into place, I packed up the Ford 4WD with camping and hunting gear and began my trek.

The long drive ended in Fairbanks, where I visited friends. I followed it with a quick trip to Valdez to try for goat. The dangerous snow, ice and bad weather opened my eyes to the "do-it-yourself dangers" and I think I was wise to pack it in early, retreating from the long goat routine to try for a black bear.

Reports when I checked up on the caribou migration said the herd was a bit behind schedule, so the two or three days of bear hunting should've filled the gap. Instead, the lack of success quickly eroded my enthusiasm for this solo safari. My hopes now were riding

Continued on page 90

My Own Knife Almost Took My Life continued from page 89

on moose as I joined my Fairbanks friends and drove to Paxson in east central Alaska. Three-wheel motorcycles took us deeper into the bush from town.

It took a week to finally catch up with a 40-inch bull, but the 30-06 was gun enough to bring him down without much trouble in the thick bush and at pretty close range. A thousand pounds of moose is no joking matter, but my buddies from Fairbanks chided me about the rack. Seems they're used to five-foot spreads up there, but us Minnesotans can appreciate the hunt no matter what the size of antlers (at least I had them believing it long enough to let me continue my hunt).

With a moose under my belt now and my success just starting, I decided it was time for my first choice animal of this Alaskan adventure.

I drove to Anchorage and hopped a flight with Air Alaska to King Salmon, from which I took Peninsula Airways about an hour south, where I set up base camp. You better believe I remembered the signal for distress would be an orange tarp spread on the ground, because when that Cherokee 6 left me alone on a short stretch of sand in the wilderness three Wyoming hunters who had used the base camp the week before were flying out with the pilot who flew me in. They had two caribou, but said the animals were pretty few and far between.

If only the caribou would come as thick as the hordes of bugs. Every breath I took I inhaled a mouthful of critters. A headnet and Muskol saved me as I set up camp near a small river close to the make-shift landing strip.

For days, I slept very little, glassed quite a lot and saw only a few distant caribou and a couple of far off brown bear; thank the lord for far off brown bear.

Days passed and the monotony and disappointment of more caribou, but few racks, finally got to me. Wind and rain beat me and the long stalks that ended in no shot because the racks were too small, all take their toll. Ptarmigan stew is somewhat satisfying, but when I was cleaning the pots the next morning real satisfaction arrived.

There, finally, across the river was a nice herd of maybe 100 caribou with at least a dozen big bulls. They were over the next ridge before I could stop staring at the huge racks. I grabbed some candy, my boots and a rifle. I'm diabetic, so the candy helps maintain my blood sugar. But I just didn't have enough energy to keep up with the herd as it reached the next ridge ahead of me. I wasn't going to give up. Ten ridges and four rivers later, I finally caught up with the herd.

I crawled up the last ridge and saw them slowly feeding about 150 yards away. The adrenaline really started to pump and it made up for the drained energy.

I sized up the bulls. Five of the bulls near the back of the herd had impressive double shovels, and deciding which one to take was tough. I finally picked one and took a deep breath.

The crosshairs came into place and I waited for the shuffling herd to clear a shot. I also made sure another caribou wasn't behind my bull because I knew the 180-grain Federal Premium load could do its job and still push the Nosler Partition bullet into another animal. Usually, though, it mushrooms just right to do the trick inside the game. I just wanted to be extra careful.

I squeezed the trigger. The sound spooked the herd toward the next ridge. My bull was with them. I lost track of him and couldn't get another shot. But then the big bull lagged behind enough and I could see he was mine. A second shot finished him off.

I was standing over him in no time. I cleaned him up and started to cape out the hide, all the while admiring the sure record book rack. That's when I made a near fatal mistake.

I exerted a little too much pressure on my knife and the blade slipped from the caribou and into my thigh. The puncture penetrated to the bone. I stood there, alone in the bush, with a bloody knife—my own knife—stuck in my leg.

Slowly, I eased the knife out, wincing from the pain, but feeling in control out of necessity maybe. I was afraid the blood would come gushing out and the wolves would have

Continued on page 92

a double treat waiting for them right where I stood over the caribou.

The thick layers of skin and muscle slid back together, but fortunately the blood never flowed freely like it would if I had pierced an artery. Here's where my hospital emergency room training paid off. I knew from the lack of blood that I didn't have to panic for the moment because I missed the major artery and veins.

I wrapped a bandanna around it as a pressure bandage and headed back for camp. Don't ask me what possessed me to do it, but I hauled them damn four-foot by four-foot antlers on my shoulders as I hobbled back to camp. I guess I felt I deserved them, and I was either aware of the fact the wound wasn't so serious or I must have figured if I was going to die, this rack would be my tombstone.

Well, I wouldn't be writing this if I didn't make it back to camp, but you can bet I was sore and tired like all get out. Happy to be "home," I stitched myself up with stuff from my first-aid kit, and put on some antibiotic salve.

Don't ask me why, but I spent the next day hobbling back and forth with caribou meat to camp. I would rest, then go back for meat.

I put out the signal for the plane to come and pick me up on its daily pass to other camps. The next day, the pilot landed and looked at me like I had just been through World War III. I knew I had him confused because I was wearing a proud smile that can only be understood by those who matched wits with wild game in its own world and came home with more than memories as a tribute to the hunt.

The satisfaction was intensified recently when my caribou scored 420⅝ points, well above the 400-point minimum for the Boone and Crockett record book.

Take Your Best "Shot"

ACROSS
1. Rifle manufacturer
5. Type of shotgun
7. German manufacturer
8. Sighting support
11. Pull the trigger
13. With 8 across
15. Breech mechanism of gun
16. Helps you see distances
19. _____ of sight
21. Needed to lubricate gun
22. Small end of scope
25. Shotgun bore sizes
27. Type of sights
28. Ram_____
29. Deer camp bed
32. Lead or steel pellets
33. Ammo manufacturer
36. In handloading: min. ___
38. Not down
39. German ejector system
41. Place for extra shells
42. Unit of sound pressure
43. Filler in a shotshell

DOWN
1. .257 namesake
2. What a boy becomes
3. Path of bullet
4. Gun owners' national organization
5. Conclusive evidence
6. Pa's mate
9. Make a shooting lane
10. Bullet passes through
12. Shells that you load yourself

14. Long gun
17. Military rank (abbr.)
18. Marine creature
20. Browning choke system
23. Determines shot pattern
24. End
24. Start
26. Therefore
30. Vigor
31. Distance in shooting
33. Walk in a line
34. To fool or trick
35. Short term for a light shoulder rifle
37. Swing a gun in advance of a moving target
40. The sun

Answers on page 188.

*Future hunter and NAHC member Aaron Berger
with his trusty BB gun*

Take Your Boy Hunting, And You'll Never Have To Hunt For Him

Bob Allen, President of Bob Allen Companies, Inc.

Most boys learn about guns, shooting and hunting
from their dads. In my case, my dad was born in
Ireland where guns and hunting are not available
to the average person. He had no knowledge of them,
whatsoever, and actually had some fear of guns.

Although my mother was an Iowa farm girl, and came from
a family that had been involved in hunting and shooting,
she went along with my dad's feelings, and as a consequence,
when as a young boy, I wanted to have a BB gun, my parents
elected to not allow me to have one until I was 12 years old.

At that point, most of my peers were graduating to .22
rifles or shotguns, and I found myself ashamed to go out in
the woods with my gun. This led me to buying a single-shot
.22 without my parents knowledge and hiding it in a hollow
tree in the woods near home so that I could start out from
the house with a BB gun, pick up the rifle, and actually do
my hunting with the .22, replacing it in the hollow tree
on my way home. My parents, in their ignorance when it
came to guns, assumed that some of the squirrels and
rabbits I shot had been killed with the BB gun.

To this day, I have a strong hunch that their reticence
in allowing me to have guns may have intensified
my desire for them; it often seems to work this way.
If parents try to keep something from their children, then
the children want it all the more.

On the other side of the coin, I had a friend whose burning
desire was to have a son and make a hunter out of him.
From the time the boy could walk, the dad dragged him
along on various outings and tried in every possible way to

continued on page 96

include the son in his outdoor plans. It didn't take, and soon the boy balked at even going out with his father, much to his dad's disappointment. As it later turned out, the boy's interests were in other things, and once his dad realized this and stopped pushing, they developed a good father/son relationship.

When my son Matt was born, naturally I had hopes that he would share my love of the outdoors. The knowledge of my friend's experience with his son, and the recollection of my own boyhood, led me to use some psychology of my own to assure that Matt would enjoy hunting with me.

I started by taking him out to the gun club with me, and I did this just part of the time. I tied it in with some weekend camping expeditions. About this state in his life, Matt was going through a period in which he was fascinated by knives, hatchets and matches. He had innocently hacked up some good trees at home already, and I was fearful what the fascination with matches might lead to, so I planned some outings where he could get it all out of his system.

On these outings, we would go first to the local gun club where Matt would accompany me to the trap or skeet field. Then we would head for a timbered area in a river bottom nearby. I would get out the hatchet and knife and let Matt vent his energy for a while in gathering firewood. Then I'd let him build the fire and we would cook hotdogs or small steaks and sit around talking about the wonders of the outdoors, hunting, etc.

We did this even in cold snowy weather, and both of us looked forward to these outings. They presented a great showcase to use in introducing Matt to all the aspects of the great outdoors. The result was just what I wanted—to whet Matt's appetite for these outdoor activities.

As he grew older, I bought him a BB gun and taught him gun safety, and also, began to teach him instinct shooting in our backyard. By the age of seven or eight, he got so he could hit small objects thrown in the air, and this became the trick-shooting act which we still perform together.

I let Matt accompany me, along with some of my friends, on a few pheasant hunts. He would carry his BB gun and work the fields with us. I told him that when I could hunt all day with him and not find myself looking down the barrel muzzle of his gun or see him do anything unsafe, then I would consider getting him a real gun.

When he was about nine years old, I bought a 28-gauge shotgun for him and had it cut down so that it just about fit him. I told him that when it did fit him properly, so that he could hold it comfortably, I would start him shooting skeet, and, possibly, hunting.

Practically every week, Matt would get the gun out of the gun cabinet and, with me watching, try to see if it fit properly. All of the time I was constantly stressing the great responsibility of handling real guns and building in him a second nature for the awareness of safety.

It wasn't too long before the 28-gauge fit him, and Matt started skeet shooting with me. After a spring and a summer of skeet, I invited him on his first hunt that fall. I was really pleased at his attitude on gun handling. He even ended up being critical of some of the gun handling habits demonstrated by my friends, and, in a few instances, justifiably so.

At age 13, Matt and I went on an African safari and hunted in Mozambique together. This turned out to be the greatest experience of both our lives, and we really came to know and respect each other. Because we were hunting dangerous game such as cape buffalo, I began treating Matt as an adult, and it really paid off. I felt that if I could turn a 13 year old boy loose in Africa with a white hunter and trackers to hunt one of the most dangerous animals in the world, he most certainly deserved treatment as a grownup. This really matured Matt, and from then on I allowed him to hunt by himself

continued on page 98

and with his friends. He always demonstrated good hunting and gun handling habits.

We've had many wonderful hunts together, and we hunt every fall. Matt has developed into a fine game shot and now shares my love of hunting—not necessarily for the shooting or the actual killing of birds and animals, but for the wonderful camaraderie, the camp life, and the exciting and beautiful world of the outdoors.

The camaraderie of a father/son hunting team just cannot be improved upon. There are few things that a father and his son can do together that weld relationships like hunting does. I've heard the late Herb Parsons, Winchester's famous exhibition shooter, say it many times, "Take your boy hunting, and you'll never have to hunt for your boy!"

Opening Day
Salvatore J. Borrelli, East Rutherford, New Jersey

It was opening day eve.
I took in a breath of cool autumn air;
My head now untroubled, my mind not a care.
All year I have waited for this moment to be;
Out here in God's country, my companions and me.
The colors of autumn are so rich you could eat them;
The laughter and joking make a real hunter's hymn.
The fireplace cracking with well seasoned wood;
Warms the soul and makes our bodies feel good.
The blaze orange vests and red checkered caps;
Belonging to me and the rest of the chaps.
On wooden pegs hung waiting for dawn;
Soon after breakfast they will be worn.

At long last morning had broke.
We rose from our sleep without use of alarms;
Legs hung from our bunks as we stretched out our arms.
Then down at the stream we washed quick as we can;
And sat down to breakfast; eggs, toast and ham.
Then from the wood pegs, grabbed our caps and our vests;
And out on the porch wished all the best.
Some to the South, the East and West;
And I to the North as I buttoned my vest.
The colors of autumn, my eyes are in awe;
My spirit uplifted at the things that I saw.
We hunted all day until almost sundown;
And soon it was time to be cabinbound.
That night at the cabin, well fed and content;
We swapped stories about how our day was spent.
We joked and talked, had an occasional gag;
And soon it was time for the old sleeping bag.
Before fading out, I took a moment to say;
'Thank you God for friends and Opening Day.'

A Cat In The Card Game

Merrill *"Mac" McCubbin*

NAHC Member's Story

After moving our gunshop and sporting goods business to Maine in the middle 1950's, my partner and I started looking for a deer campsite in the "Puckerbrush Country," as the "downeasteners" would say. We finally got one from St. Regis Paper Company. It was located in Mancock County, and far back.

Not being able to fix up the old hovel for a camp until near deer season in mid October, we went in about a week before to fix it up. Getting there a little before dark, all we could get done was the roof, so we could at least sleep dry.

After supper, we all gathered around a blanket spread on the old board floor for a little game of stud poker before sack time. You can't use dogs to hunt deer in Maine—then or now—but at that time both bobcat and black bear were classed as vermin and a $15.00 bounty was paid on them. Some hunters in the area had cat and bear dogs and, at that time, dogs just ran as they pleased in the wilderness areas.

A little after dark, we heard a couple of dogs baying as they passed at what sounded about a hundred yards away. We wondered what they were after.

The game continued for perhaps an hour, and we were on the last hand and last beer when, suddenly, something came sailing through the one window opening and landed in the middle of our makeshift card table blanket. It was a medium-sized bobcat. And believe me, gentlemen, that card game broke up in one helluva hurry!

One second there were five men seated around that blanket, and a cat in the middle. The next second that cabin was as empty as an old maid's arms. We all went out the nearest exit, and after looking the shack over the next day, I think someone made some new ones. It seems the cat lived under the fallen lean-to kitchen and had just returned home from the race with the hounds.

Now, I have hunted all over this country, but never have I had a greater surprise than that cat almost landing in my lap!

Name That Cartridge

1. Many young hunters shoot this cartridge their very first time shooting. As popular for plinking tin cans on the farm as it is for shooting squirrels in the woods.
   _____

2. A very popular varmint cartridge, this has been used extensively in the military guised as the 5.56mm.
   _____

3. Developed in 1955, this flat shooting cartridge works well for larger varmints, deer and antelope if using the right bullets. _____

4. An excellent cartridge for shooting deer-sized game, this was Jack O'Connor's all time favorite. _____

5. There was a time when two out of every three horses on the trail had a Winchester Model 94 carbine in this caliber hung in its saddle. Historically, the most popular deer hunting cartridge of all time. _____

6. The standard by which all other big-game rifle cartridges are judged, this extremely popular cartridge is readily available in a huge variety of bullet weights and has a fine reputation for hunting big game._____

7. This flat shooting magnum has a reputation for sure, quick long-range killing of big game like elk. It began as the 7x57 Mauser military round in 1892._____

8. This magnum has a velocity edge on all other .30 caliber cartridges. It was introduced to the commercial market in about 1948 by the legendary man named Roy.
   _____

9. A very versatile cartridge for heavy game under nearly any condition. A 200-grain bullet in this caliber is listed at 3,000 fps. This magnum was unveiled by Winchester in 1958 and quickly attained classic status. _____

10. Originally made in England in both belted and rimmed versions for use in bolt-action and double rifles, this cartridge is the most popular magnum for game of all sizes from deer to elephants._____

Answers are on page 190.

20 Tips For
Close To Home Trophy Bucks
Jeff Murray

For most hunters, talk of a dream trip for a trophy whitetail to Alberta, or an extra season across the border remains just that: talk. The reason is, of course, that all of us are on strictly budgeted time schedules. The gap between talking about an extended hunt and doing it is wider than Washington can toss a coin across.

And those few who do manage to pull off such a trip more often than not return with a severe case of the wait-until-next-year blues. Having big bucks around you is one thing. Killing one is another matter. It seems that just when a hunter gets to know an area well enough to move in for the kill, it's time to go home.

Big bucks are different, and it takes time to figure them out. That's why average hunters using average tactics will generally score on average deer.

Just suppose time wasn't a problem. And suppose you've got bucks with decent racks close by. What would your odds be for scoring on that buck of a lifetime? Very good, to say the least. One of the big stories in the world of whitetail deer hunting has been all the trophies that are being taken within commuting distance of "lucky" hunters.

Hunting close to home, however, takes as much skill as an out-of-town adventure. In fact, it takes more planning, and more grit to be successful at it. Yet I've seen scores of good hunters blow it. Below is a rundown of some areas I know that harbor bucks. Apply the generalities locally, and see if you don't agree.

1 *Special hunts.* Each fall, special lottery-type hunts are organized for public lands to "keep the deer numbers in check." At the top of the list are state parks and state and national wildlife refuges. Some support a limited hunting season every year, while others

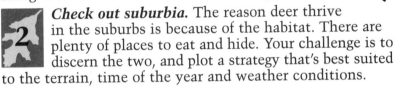

are only open when the park manager, or district offices, deem it appropriate.

The key is to be on top of the situation and not let one slip by unnoticed. A good way to avoid this is to cultivate a relationship with field personnel in order to stay on top of game trends.

Also, collect game regulations (the booklets you receive when you buy a hunting license). They list these "extra" hunts along with deadlines and addresses for applications.

Check out suburbia. The reason deer thrive in the suburbs is because of the habitat. There are plenty of places to eat and hide. Your challenge is to discern the two, and plot a strategy that's best suited to the terrain, time of the year and weather conditions.

A shortcut to this process is the little-known soil conservation map. These maps indicate soil types, drainage patterns and watersheds. This is where most of the deer will be, and by overlaying an aerial photograph with a good soil map, logical hotspots will emerge.

Consider golf courses. The local golf course is a great place for a buck to hang around. Witness Bill Kontras' No. 2 Pope & Young monster. It was a links junkie because the early green shoots in the spring, the cover and an abundant source of water made life easy.

Surprisingly, greens keepers hate deer and might accommodate your plea to hunt their lands. Deer, you see, ruin plush fairways and greens with their sharp hooves, and eat sprouting vegetation. It's possible to get permission to hunt a golf course, but it won't be easy (safety and liability are the main concerns). Don't fret. Ask adjoining property owners.

Scour river bottoms. Most deer stay where they ought to, and a lush river bottom will always be at the top of their list, when available. Food doubles as security cover, so what more could a whitetail want?

Problem is, most hunters know this, and competition

continued on page 104

can be tough. Select an access point that's slightly out of
the way.

Hunt from a fence. Top bowhunter Myles Keller
uses the too-obvious-but-always-overlooked fenceline to great advantage. There's a reason nobody has
taken more Pope & Young trophies than Keller, and
fencelines are an integral part of his strategy.

"From a fenceline I can 'pre-hunt' while I'm scouting,"
he says. "I have a full 360-degree field of view, and the
bonus of a buck every so often is hard to beat."

Keller chooses fencelines judiciously. He prefers those
that string out from woodlots, but also bisect row crops.
Deer are more likely to use them than those that have no
nearby cover.

Hunt food plots. Minnesota's best
whitetail came from a 20-acre
cornfield. And why not? The
deer was undisturbed for three
years. The corn provided an ideal day-
time bedding lair.

But hunting corn is hardly a panacea.
Where do you put up a stand? How do you
see? Smart hunters have learned to look for
sign on treelines bordering such food plots,
then erect a stand that's strategically located
to cover the treeline and cornfield.

Discover a swamp island and hunt it hard.
Swamps, like lakes, look pretty uniform on the
surface. But with a critical eye, it's amazing what
irregularities you'll find. A swamp island is the
perfect counterpart to a reef in a lake.

Swamp islands can be found with topo maps. First,
locate swamps with the marsh symbol. Then look for small
circles or doughnut-shaped double-circles within the marsh.
The lines on a topo map connect points of equal elevation,
and the circles tell you where there's a little knoll.

What makes swamp islands so attractive to bucks is an
obvious reprieve from hunter pressure; few hunters know
about them, and even fewer hunt them. But forget about

hunting them if the wind isn't perfect. The deer will scent you and likely abandon the island.

 Don't drive by highway corridors. One Halloween night I almost hit the biggest deer I'd ever seen. It was standing broadside in the middle of an interstate highway when my lights reflected off its eyes. Undaunted, it ambled into the woods. After I carefully marked the spot, I returned the following week, to find a stretch of land laced with deer sign.

For some reason, hunters think that deer only live off of dirt roads. Not so. If you take the time to scout lands along freeways and four-laners, you'll find plenty of deer and very few hunters.

 Find a private woodlot adjacent to public lands. If I could pick one landowner to befriend, this is the one I'd choose. Deer don't care if land is public or private, but they do know where the fewest hunters are.

Better yet, knock on the door of privately-owned tracts within a heavily hunted wildlife management unit. If food plots are close by, all the better. But when you ask, look civil. Don't come in camo clothing. Wear a dress shirt and maybe a tie. I like to bring my 10-year-old son, Jared, along on occasion. These folks need to know that hunters are real people with real jobs and real families — just like them.

 Hunt a wildlife management area on the pheasant opener. I still remember it like it was yesterday. It was 1981, opening day of pheasant season. Glowing predictions for a great bird season sent shotgunners marching abreast through shoulder-high cover. I was one of them.

But when I reached the end of a shelterbelt that formed a neat "T" with a ditchbank, I wasn't thinking of roosters. A bowhunter was about to put a knife to the paunch of a dandy 10-point buck. We had pushed the deer to the hunter, and it was no accident.

"Happens almost every year," he confessed reluctantly. "You have to be quick, though."

continued on page 106

Make efficiency your main ally. To do this, set up a milk run of hotspots that can be hit one by one. That way, you'll avoid hop-scotching all over the countryside, dictated by last moment whims and fancies.

 Plot each area on a map. This will give you the big picture, as well as the most logical travel routes. The perfect map for this is a township fire map. It isn't too cluttered with detail, like the individual maps you might want to construct for each spot, but it has enough information to keep you on track. If fire maps aren't available, use county highway maps.

 Invest in high-power binoculars. They aren't just for Western hunts. When I obtained a pair of Steiner 15X80s, I soon discovered that a lengthy, tedious scouting ordeal can be less painful and more effective. The price is worth it when you consider that you can watch deer totally undetected, without them knowing you're on the same planet.

By "high-power" I'm referring to optics with a magnification between 15 and 20. You will need a tripod, however, but today's lightweight aluminum models fold down to a compact 3- by 14- inch rectangle. The window of your vehicle, rolled up a bit, will also provide stability.

 Visit each area regularly. By checking every spot personally, you'll be able to keep tabs on sudden shifts in deer movements. You know that there's no substitute for being in the right place at the right time, and this is the best way to do it.

 Use a buddy system. Obviously, a little help from one of your friends can go a long way toward accomplishing the above goals. Two guys can split up the chores of field work, after dividing the hunting territory into zones.

For example, if your partner lives closer to several key spots, let him monitor them. And when an area or two gets hot, you can double up.

 Consider baiting where legal and practical. Nothing can tell you as much about a new area as fast as a prudent ration of cracked corn. If you fail to generate a lot of whitetail activity within a couple of days, move on. But be sure to check state regulations before baiting.

 Ask the right people. The milk man, propane gas man and UPS driver can save you a lot of time. They travel rural areas on a regular basis, covering their beat as thoroughly as anyone. If a deer with a decent rack dwells in a certain area, chances are one of these individuals will see it.

 Hunt the rut harder than the rest of the year. Every fall I watch hunters burn themselves out prematurely. Just when it's time to deliver a knock-out punch, they don't have anything to give. They sleep in and have a hard time concentrating. There is no antidote, just preventive medicine: Avoid spreading yourself too thin, get needed rest, and be ready for action.

 Carry your hunting gear with you at all times. I stash mine in doubled-sealed plastic trash bags. They're in the back of the pickup whether I'm going to church or to the store. You never know when a buck might appear in the open for a close shot. It happens, and you need to be ready.

 Hunt the same hotspots over the years. Eventually, patterns emerge. For reasons only God knows, deer exhibit certain behavior in certain locales. Only experience will show you what it is.

And when you invest time in your own backyard, you won't have to listen to, "You should have been here last week."

Reprinted from **North American Hunter Deer Spectacular,** *Volume 2, 1989.*

Dive-Bombing Bluebills

Dan D. Gapen Sr.

They came as they had for countless decades, homing flocks of bluebills responding to that ancestral instinct to migrate. Their November flight south was again taking them over the North Dakota-Manitoba border. And it was again taking them over Border Lake and our blind.

Far to the north, an erratic line was materializing. At first its coming and going was blurred. Then, as if by magic, the line solidified and became a faintly waving string comprised of numerous bluebills. To the west, another line, this one shorter. And between these two flocks, a faint pair of dots. We watched. The pair was moving at a good clip, so we hunkered down in the blind, intent on their flight path.

This is a ritual for me, hunting these waters just before the big winter freeze. It's my last fast shooting of the year, something that gets my blood pumping fast enough to carry me through the Minnesota winter.

This year I was hunting with Dan Stewart and Jim Riemersma. Dan and I were on one point, and Jim was on a point 100 yards to our left. Bluebills came screaming down the shoreline, zipping at neck-snapping speed right before our blinds.

We hunkered a little lower.

The approaching bluebills were no more than 200 yards away. Knowing they would pass right in front of us, Dan whispered, "I'll take the one on the left." Jim would get a shot if one snuck through.

Simultaneously, Dan and I pulled up, swung with the birds and slapped off our shots. Mine tucked and tumbled to the water. My lab Wapsi dashed in to retrieve.

Dan's, meanwhile, wobbled, rolled and then glided toward Jim's blind. "Good," I thought, "with Waldo my other lab holding at Jim's side, there'll be no lost cripple."

Jim was already standing up, and he pulled up on the descending duck, and let loose a shot. The bluebill took the punch from Jim's shot and puffed some feathers. But it raced on, right at Jim's blind.

As the sound of the shot reached us, Jim was punched out of his blind. He fell back and thumped into the muck and cattails.

Dan and I looked at each other, bewildered. Waldo, sitting in Jim's blind, picked up the bluebill, looked back at Jim laying in the cattails and then looked across at Dan and me.

"Hey Jim, you alright?" I called. We heard moans, but no answer. "Hey Jim, what happened?"

We tried to peer over the cattails, but they were too high.

We heard more moans, and then silence.

Dan and I again looked at each other. Instantly, he hopped into the boat, pulled the starter cord hard and twisted the throttle.

Had my friend's gun blown up in his face? Had one of his handloads been too hot?

In no time, Dan was at the other blind. I watched as he bumped into the cattails, cut the engine and hopped out of the boat. He crouched down in the weeds, and I heard his muffled comments and questions.

I called over, several times, but he didn't answer. Again I considered the possibilities. I looked at his blind, trying to visualize what had happened. Waldo, still in the blind, looked back at me, bluebill in mouth, obediently waiting for a "good boy".

"Gapen!" came a yell. I waited. "He's okay; just had the wind knocked out of him."

Dan helped Jim to his feet, and steadied him for a few minutes as he got his bearings back. The duck had smacked him square in the chest. He had a nasty bruise to show for it.

We hunted out the rest of the day. Dan and I had a fine afternoon, but Jim seemed a bit timid whenever a bluebill came screaming in.

—R. STUBLER—

"You and your stupid shortcuts!"

·THE GREAT· Whitetail Quiz

Part Five

Part Five of this enjoyable quiz is sure to test your knowledge of whitetail hunting facts. When you're ready for more, turn to pages 136-137 for Part Six.

51) In many states the number of deer killed annually on highways:
A. Nearly equals the gun harvest.
B. Exceeds the bow harvest.
C. Is insignificant.

52) Methods of estimating deer populations include:
A. Analysis of harvest history.
B. Pellet group surveys.
C. Sex-Age-Kill data.
D. All of the above.

53) The factor that most affects individual hunter success is:
A. Deer density in the area hunted.
B. Buck-to-doe ratio in the area hunted.
C. Hunter familiarity with the area and deer habits.

54) When using a masking agent to cover human scent, the hunter should use:
A. As strong an odor as possible.
B. A natural scent.
C. A deer lure.

55) When using a buck lure, the lure should be placed:
A. On hunting clothes.
B. On the ground around the stand.
C. On a piece of tissue or cloth and placed within shooting distance.

56) As a general rule, when a deer herd is at the carrying capacity, the deer herd can be maintained at this level with an anteriess harvest as high as:
A. 20 percent of the legal buck harvest.
B. 40 percent of the legal buck harvest.
C. 60 percent of the legal buck harvest.
D. 80 percent of the legal buck harvest.

57) Game managers are more concerned with:
A. Trends; increases and decreases in the deer population.
B. Actual number of deer.

58) Deer hunting is a:
A. Right; B. Privilege.

59) The factor which usually has the greatest influence on deer movement patterns during the deer gun season is:
A. Hunting pressure.
B. Weather conditions.
C. Deer food preferences.

60) Posting of private land is frequently the result of:
A. Selfish landowners.
B. Hunter misconduct.
C. Attempts to prevent an overharvest of game animals.

61) The majority of bucks harvested by deer hunters are:
A. Less than 2.5 years old.
B. 2.5 to 3.5 years old.
C. 3.5 years old or older.

62) When starvation occurs in the winter months, which deer are affected first:
A. Bucks
B. Does
C. Fawns

Answers are on page 185.

"Best lure I ever tried."

Attacked By A Bear

Jeff Tausch, Corning, California

My son and I were on a 1994 archery deer hunt when this took place. We hunt southern Trinity County in Northern California. That morning we had decided to split up, using a spot and stalk type of hunting.

About two hours into the hunt I spotted a 300 to 350 pound bear in the trail. I stopped and watched him for a few minutes. The bear wouldn't move as he watched me. We were about 75 yards apart.

I looked around for an escape route. There wasn't any that was practical. Then I stood up and yelled at the bear.

The bear then charged me, coming within 10 feet, slamming his paws on the ground and growling. When I tried to back away from him, he became aggressive. He then charged again, this time putting his left shoulder into my right thigh and pushing on me.

My thoughts at this time were, "This is it. He's going to take me." Then I remembered a TV program that showed what to do if attacked by a bear.

When the bear backed away about two feet I laid my bow down, got down on my knees in a fetal-type position, covering my head and eyes. The bear approached me, sniffing my back, then pushing with his nose at my arms and head. He then made a woof sound and ran off!

Sounds incredible, doesn't it! Believe me, it only took me about 15 minutes to get back to camp.

★★★★★★★★★★★★★★★★★★★★★★★★★★★★★★★★★★★★★★

A country preacher was out hunting squirrels one fall afternoon. Hearing a noise behind him, he turned and found a big bear reared up on its hind legs. Knowing his small .22 would only make the bear meaner, he dropped to his hands and knees and prayed, "Lord, save me from this bear."

He looked up and the bear was even closer. He prayed, "Lord, let this be a Christian bear."

When he looked up again the bear was hunkered down praying, "Lord, bless this food which I am about to receive ..."

"Sam... wanna go hunting?"

The Big Gun Word Search

```
M  A  R  L  I  N  A  L  W  A  Y  S  K  E  E
P  W  Y  A  M  E  R  I  C  A  N  A  R  M  S
O  E  U  R  M  U  Z  Z  L  E  S  A  K  O  S
S  A  N  O  T  G  N  I  M  E  R  P  O  M  I
M  T  N  T  E  G  D  I  N  A  I  S  R  R  A
I  H  A  F  E  D  R  I  R  L  E  A  C  E  T
T  E  T  I  O  N  K  E  L  E  A  E  P  T  T
H  R  R  U  G  E  R  E  B  T  Y  O  U  S  E
&  B  R  G  U  S  N  N  O  S  U  N  L  E  R
W  Y  O  A  K  N  D  K  E  D  S  W  H  H  E
E  E  N  B  E  N  A  O  T  I  N  O  U  C  B
S  S  E  B  T  D  H  I  N  K  T  S  M  N  A
S  F  B  R  O  W  N  I  N  G  E  L  T  I  Y
O  A  L  S  A  V  A  G  E  E  X  S  O  W  G
N  M  A  G  N  U  M  R  E  S  E  A  R  C  H
```

AMERICAN ARMS	REMINGTON
BENNELLI	RUGER
BERETTA	SAKO
BROWNING	SAVAGE
COLT	SKB
DAKOTA ARMS	SMITH&WESSON
MAGNUM RESEARCH	WEATHERBY
MARLIN	WINCHESTER
MOSSBERG	

Answers are on page 186.

Roy E. Weatherby
Founder of Weatherby, Inc.

Celebrity Chef

Elk, Venison or Moose Oven Burgundy

Serves: 6 to 8
Prep Time: 3½ hours

2 tablespoons soy sauce
2 tablespoons flour
2 pounds venison, elk or moose stew meat
4 carrots, cut into chunks
2 large onions, thinly sliced
1 cup celery, thinly sliced
1 minced garlic clove
¼ teaspoon pepper
¼ teaspoon marjoram
¼ teaspoon thyme
1 cup burgundy, or any dry red wine
1 cup sliced mushrooms

Blend soy sauce and flour in 3-qt. baking dish. Cut meat into 1½-inch cubes. Add to soy sauce mixture; toss to coat.

Add the cut-up carrots, sliced onions and celery, minced garlic, pepper, marjoram, thyme and wine to the meat. Stir gently to mix. Cover tightly and oven simmer at 325° for two hours.

Add mushrooms and again stir gently. Cover tightly and bake one hour longer— or until meat and vegetables are tender. Serve with fluffy hot wild rice, noodles or mashed potatoes.

He is a legend, for his designs and innovations in the firearms field have changed the entire industry. Many experts claim he has accomplished more in the arms industry than any other man in generations. Since starting in business in 1945, his products have gained a reputation of quality and prestige second to none.

His interest in guns and hunting started at the age of six as a farm boy in Kansas. He and his wife moved to California in 1937 and he became a successful insurance salesman. In 1945 he gave up his lucrative career and entered the gun business with nothing but a knowledge of guns and ballistics, coupled with a lot of ideas, enthusiasm, perseverance and tremendous ambition.

Today, Weatherby, Inc. manufactures sporting firearms, scopes and related accessories. Ed Weatherby is Chairman of the Board, making Weatherby one of the few remaining family-owned gun companies with a history that now spans three generations.

Then Came Success

Norman Truelove

The two does startled me when they bounded from their beds only 100 yards from me. My heart jumped, but my permit said "Buck only!" I lowered my gun and watched them wave good-bye with their big white tails.

Deer season is an exciting time for our family. My dad takes his vacation from work and my uncle cuts his farming chores to a minimum. I, unfortunately, hunt only the weekends because I'm still in school.

All of our deer hunting is done on the farm land surrounding our home in Hartford, Kansas. During the first two days of the season, I spent hours sitting in a hedge tree on my uncle's farm. A creek with plenty of timber for cover passes through the farm and deer often go through the area in the mornings and evenings.

Opening day, a six-pointer passed within 100 yards of me. Cold weather, a twitchy finger and plenty of excitement all resulted in a complete miss! The deer turned and started running straight for the tree I was sitting in. He turned broadside about 50 feet away. I shot again, but missed a second time.

I was very upset with myself by that time. I did manage to stay in the tree and watch the deer moving to the east. I noticed my uncle coming across the field. He spotted the buck and snapped off a shot as it disappeared. He also missed. Both of us headed back to the house for food and warmth, and to share our misery.

The second day of the season was a complete bust. We hunted the same area but, contrary to our hopes, the buck didn't show himself again. I was disheartened. I had to go back to school in the morning and wouldn't be able to hunt until late in the afternoon. Still, it was good to get out of the bitter wind that plagued us all day.

As predicted, my classroom work received very little

attention the next day. During first hour, I kept thinking about the six-pointer I missed. I spent the next two planning my afternoon hunt. Hours three and four were spent reliving a great shot I made on a monster buck that lives in the back of my mind. I started at the clock for the last hour. I wanted to get a buck!

When the dismissal bell rang, I hurdled my desk and headed out the door at top speed. At home, I quickly changed into my hunting clothes and grabbed my rifle. My uncle was waiting for me.

We decided to try another area to the south. My uncle had seen several deer there while harvesting several weeks earlier. I was so wired by the time we made it into the timber, my heart nearly stopped when we jumped two does on the way to our stands. Our permits were good for bucks only, so we had to let them go. We knew the does had blown our cover for the day and were sure that our chances of seeing a buck were slim, but we continued on anyway.

There was only one hour of legal hunting time remaining by the time we selected our stands. I chose an old walnut on the west side of a draw. My uncle found a hedge tree southeast of me and on the opposite side of the draw. Half an hour went by. Nothing showed but a bunch of woodpeckers, bluejays and squirrels. Suddenly an enormous buck appeared—and he was heading straight toward the tree I was in! I immediately raised my rifle to my shoulder. The buck must have spotted me because he froze and stared in my direction. I took advantage of the situation and hurriedly squeezed the trigger. The buck wheeled and bounded away in a frantic retreat.

"Did you hit him?" my uncle hollered.

"I should have," I yelled back as I scrambled down the tree.

continued on page 118

We met where the buck was standing when I shot. There was no blood or hair in the immediate area, but I felt good about my shot. We started following the buck's tracks. We found the first pool of blood 50 feet later. It sent my heart into my throat. We continued on. Rounding the next thicket I spotted him. The biggest buck I had ever seen was laying in the grass in front of me. My dream had come true!

All the frustration of opening day was forgotten in seconds. My uncle slapped me on the back, congratulating me on a fine shot. The story telling began.

Uncle Earl had seen the buck first and, unknown to me, had been following the buck in his sights. The buck stopped when he apparently heard my uncle move into a better shooting position. Lucky for me, the buck was in my sights by that time. He was hidden from my uncle's view by a tree.

"Three more steps and he would have been mine," Earl informed me. Excitement runs very high at a time like this!

My uncle stayed with the buck while I drove the two miles to get my dad. Dad knew when I came flying down the road, horn blaring, that I had shot a deer. After a month and a half of bowhunting himself, Dad was ready to get in on the action.

The three of us then dragged the carcass to the waiting pickup. Upon arrival at the locker plant, we found the carcass was too big for them to weigh without completely dressing it. The dressed carcass weighed 152 pounds. We also found a bowhunter's broadhead in the buck's front shoulder blade, but it apparently didn't bother him much. Some other hunter must have faced the same disappointment I had on opening day. Unlike him, I had a second chance and wound up with a winning buck.

Shoot Straight

For several years my marriage would almost end every fall when hunting season began. My wife would give me the "Honey we never do anything together all you think about is hunting." So last year I bought her a new rifle. When I got home I said, "Honey this year you're going hunting with me." After a few practice sessions the season was here. Opening morning of deer season we were ready. I instructed my wife to take the left side of the mountain and I'd go around the right side; eventually we'd meet on the far side. I hadn't gone 200 or 300 yards when I heard *BANG BANG, BANG* coming from the direction my wife had gone. I rushed there, all excited. When I got there I saw she had her gun pointed at a guy who was scared to death yelling "OK lady it's your buck, only let me get my saddle off him."

David H. Pike, Black Canyon City, AZ

Can you unscramble the names of these cartridge case types, and match them to the proper drawing?

CLETONKTEB

THASTIGR

MIDMER

Answers are on page 190.

Beating The Odds

Jeff Boehler

"Nine times out of ten" are the odds Phil Campbell uses when describing the likelihood of upcoming events...both good and bad. Phil is a true mountain man, not only at home, but in his element when in the middle of grizzly country at 10,000 feet. He is a Wyoming resident and a good friend, generous enough to go elk hunting with two "dudes" from Minnesota. Little did we know when we left our suburban homes and headed west that we would beat Phil's "nine times out of ten" odds on a number of occasions...both good and bad.

Doug McDougal and I had been planning and waiting for this trip since that glorious day in March when we found envelopes from the Wyoming Game and Fish department in our mailboxes. Our first stroke of luck was receiving elk tags the first year we applied. After six months of purchasing needed gear, running, lifting weights, reading elk books, sighting in rifles, creating equipment lists, planning menus, packing, re-packing and dreaming of bugling bulls, we loaded the truck, trailer and drove west.

After an 18 hour drive and a memorable 3 hour horseback trail ride, we arrived in a scenic mountain meadow that we would call home for the next week. We took care of the horses, grabbed a snack and headed up to the ridge to glass the valley beyond before dark. We didn't see any elk, but tracks and rubs were clearly visible, the elk were there. Tomorrow was opening day.

I'm not sure if it was from the altitude, the upcoming hunt or fresh grizzly tracks we found around our camp, but sleep wasn't easy that night. Both Doug and I were nauseous when we rose in the morning, certain it was from the altitude. Doug won the flip for first shot, we were to take turns daily based on that toss of the coin.

Knowing the ridge we were on the night before was to be hunted by another party, Phil led us to a string of meadows that hugged the side of the mountain. Doug sat on the edge of the first meadow, Phil and I walked quietly to the edge of the next. We chose a spot in the timber and sat down, anticipating a long wait. We hadn't been there 30 minutes

when we heard
shots from the top of
the ridge. First came a
minor rumble in the timber
above, then the sound of crashing
twigs and branches and a thunderous
stampede of hooves beating the ground. "Git ready, " was
all Phil had time to say. One by one, in single file, cow elk
came pouring out of the timber and into the open meadow.
One...two...three...I lost count...they came sprinting
past...straight downhill...where's the bull? There was a
short gap and then out he ran. At first I couldn't find him
in my scope, and he wasn't slowing. But then I found him,
followed him and squeezed the trigger. I don't remember
working the bolt but when he turned to follow the cows
around a giant pine tree, I shot again, at his other side. He
showed himself on the other side of the tree, I didn't have

continued on page 122

121

time to squeeze off another round, but in the scope I saw my shots had found their mark.

"Let's git after him!" Phil said excitedly. We walked quickly toward the last place we saw the big bull. There in the snow was fresh blood, my eyes followed the tracks and then I saw one of his perfectly symmetrical 6x6 antlers towering up from the ground. Twenty yards away, laying silent in the snow, was the "herd bull." Phil and I looked at each other with Cheshire Cat smiles and I shook his hand...twice.

Photos, field dressing, quartering and caping took us the rest of the morning. After a relaxing lunch in the warm mountain sun Phil and I decided to head back to camp for the mules. "Nine times out of ten bears won't come in on a fresh kill until it gets dark," reassured Phil when Doug asked him about the likelihood of bears coming in on the elk carcass. Doug and I had reason to be skeptical, there was bear sign everywhere around us, and in the past six months we had both read the tragic grizzly attack stories in *North American Hunter*. Doug stayed to watch for more elk. Like any respectable hunter during the slow midday sun, he put his head on a log, pulled his cap over his eyes and took a nap.

He awoke to the heavy sound of running feet and a rhythmic "woof...woof...woof." Thinking it was Phil and I returning with the mules he looked down towards the bottom of the meadow. In a split second he realized that the sound was coming from the trees behind him. Looking over his shoulder he spotted a grizzly bear running down

122

the mountain right at him. He grabbed his bear spray, which he had thoughtfully placed on his chest before dozing off, and stood up. The bear was less than 30 yards away and closing fast. Doug stood his ground, realizing there were no other options. He flipped the safety cap off the bear spray and prepared to defend himself; there wasn't time to grab the Browning .338 A-bolt laying on the log. Luckily, the bear was just as surprised to see Doug and immediately stopped, turned and ran back up the hill. Doug then picked up his gun and backed into the meadow, expecting the bear to return. Little did he know that there were two more grizzlies already in the meadow near the elk carcass. At that moment, Phil and I returned with the mules. Leroy, the lead mule, brayed and scared off the bears. I ran into the clearing with my gun ready; thankfully all the bears were gone. Doug stood in the meadow, and looking at me with wild eyes he yelled "BEAR! BEAR!"

It took some time for Doug to settle down enough to tell us exactly what happened. We pieced together the details and realized that Doug was actually caught in between the sow grizzly and one of her large cubs (the cubs were almost full grown). The sow and one cub were already in the meadow closing in on the kill when the other one, hearing the dinner bell, almost ran over Doug to catch up. Some questions still remained unanswered. How close to Doug did the bears enter the meadow while he was napping? Would the result of the ordeal have been different if we hadn't returned right after Doug scared off mama bear's number two cub? We were just happy to still see Doug in one piece.

On day two we were up at 5:30, the water pail was iced over. As Phil put the coffee pot on the fire grate we heard cow elk calling in the trees just behind our tent. In the dark we loaded our day packs with snacks and our day's water supply and headed up the mountain to our south. Thankfully for us flatlanders, we climbed slowly and quietly (not counting my heavy panting). We stopped to glass the opposite slopes once, and used a cow call occasionally. When we reached the plateau, two hours after we began, we sat in the snow and glassed again for any sign of another herd.

While Doug and I searched the opposite slopes, Phil spotted a herd down in the valley directly below us. A nice 5x5 was

continued on page 124

BOEHLER 97

Beating The Odds continued from page 123

with the cows, but Doug could not get set up in time to confidently take the 350+ yard shot before the bull was lost in the timber. We would not see any more elk this day but there was a lot of elk sign up there, and best of all, no sign from any other hunting parties. Phil, Doug and I had a nice leisurely lunch in the midday mountain sun. It felt like being in "God's amphitheater," we were on top of a mountain at 10,000 feet with spectacular ranges towering over us on all sides. I remember thinking "it just doesn't get any better than this." That lunch was one of my favorite memories of the trip, I hope I don't forget it any time soon.

On Thursday, day three of our hunt, Phil was going to spend a very long day packing out my elk. Doug and I were going to try and capitalize on our "vast" two days of elk hunting experience to try and take a bull for Doug on our own. I'm sure Phil was just hoping we wouldn't hurt ourselves or get lost.

We climbed the same mountain as the day before. My lungs protested as Doug led us quickly up to the top. We did our best to be perfectly quiet and Doug used the cow call as we neared the top. Elk sign; tracks, droppings and rubs were everywhere.

The mountain flattens at its peak and the trees open up into a picturesque meadow. We crunched quietly through the snow and motioned to each other when we spotted the perfect location to sit and wait. Almost exactly in the middle of this meadow there was a clump of scrubby trees with an opening tailor made for two hunters. Here we would be able to see for a hundred yards in each direction. We silently removed our day packs and settled down for a long wait...or so we thought.

The sun was blindingly bright off the patches of snow, the air was crisp and so still you could have heard a pin drop on the next ridge. Not more than ten minutes passed when I heard something off to our left. It was a faint huffing and crunching sound. Looking in that direction I almost didn't believe what I saw. All I could see over the gnarled tree trunk was antlers, glistening and slowly moving in the morning sun. I motioned to Doug, whose view was blocked by the tree trunk, to pick up his gun while I mouthed just one word: "bull." In the blink of an eye, he put the .338 to his shoulder, peeked over the tree and pulled the trigger. The elk dropped in its tracks. It was a massive 6x6 bull, with thick tines. He was definitely king of this hill. We celebrated, then spent the next four hours dressing and quartering. Doug used the knife, I stood guard with the rifle. We both agreed, once close call with grizzlies was enough for this trip.

We were grinning from ear to ear when Phil returned to camp with the horses and mules in the dark that night. We filled him in on the events of the day at the campfire during supper.

So there we were, two out-of-state "dudes" drawing Wyoming elk tags on their first try, hunting with a good friend (not a paid guide), taking two trophy elk in three days on public land, and escaping unscathed from a close encounter with three grizzly bears. Nine times out of ten that just wouldn't happen...thanks Phil!

"Go ahead and field dress it,
haul it back to the truck and I'll tidy up camp..."

★★★★★★★★★★★★★★★★★★★★★★★★★★★★★★★★★★★★★★

Two hunting buddies were going bear hunting. They got a late start, so when they got to their cabin, to save time one went in to clean the cabin while the other went to scout for bear sign.

While hunting for sign the hunter found some fresh tracks. He started to follow the tracks, and he was watching them so close he didn't notice the bear until he was face-to-face with him.

The hunter turned and ran back toward the cabin with the bear close behind. The bear was so close he could feel his breath on his back. When the hunter got to the cabin he tried to jump the steps but tripped and fell. The bear was so close and going so fast that he ran right over the hunter and in the cabin door. Thinking fast, the hunter jumped up and pulled the cabin door shut. He yelled in to his buddy, "You skin that one while I go find another one."

–Allen Frye, Saltville, Virginia

Be Prepared

Leo Gonnering, Herlong, California

Through the years I have learned, the most essential item a hunter can keep with them at all times, is a knapsack or fanny pack to carry survival items to last until rescue. It seems we never imagine ourselves falling and breaking a leg, having car trouble, getting lost, having a friend forget to pick us up, etc. Yet, this sort of thing happens every year to thousands of us. The survival pack idea is not new, however, what the pack should contain (in my opinion) may be new to your readership.

While bow hunting for black bear in Alaska, I was the victim of unfortunate circumstances that forced me to prepare for a cold, wet night on the banks of the sparsely populated Yetna River. At 4:15 p.m., I exited the boat to hike to my stand. The boat would return for me at 10:30 p.m. The plan was to drop off a hunter at the lowermost (or uppermost) stand and continue to drop hunters along the river until the last hunter parked the boat near their stand. It worked for years.

The weather was nasty. Cold north winds and heavy downpours had me shivering in my stand within 45 minutes. I was the first hunter positioned in the uppermost stand which meant I would be the first to finish hunting in the evening. This was our "first in first out" rule. I exited my stand at 10:10 p.m., wet to the bone, but quite content. I would leave the woods within minutes while my less fortunate hunting companions would wait until close to midnight. Time crept so slowly. I thought my watch was going backwards. Finally, it was 10:30 and I heard no boat. Fifteen minutes later, I could not see through the driving rain across the river less than a few hundred yards wide. I felt crushed. Something bad must have happened. Here I would remain until morning. What should I to do first? I was shivering and wet so the logical conclusion was to build a fire in the pouring rain and gusting wind. I first gathered some dry (ha) evergreen tree boughs from the bases of some mature trees and flicked my Bic to get them lit. Three flicks later my drenched Bic refused to work and I had no fire to show for my efforts. It was then that I reached into my survival pack and extracted some items an

continued on page 128

old Alaskan "Sourdough" had told me might save my life. I removed some plastic film canisters, a flint, part of an old bicycle tire and an old knife from my pack. Within a minute, I had a small fire going. Ten minutes later, I had a nice fire going which later threatened to set the tree, under which I huddled, ablaze. What was the trick? No trick, just a good survival pack weighing less than a few pounds (not including the water).

M y survival kit happens to be a fleece, waterproof fanny pack. In it I store food, fire starting materials, spare knife, survival blanket, signaling mirror, water purification tablets, steel or honing stone, spare compass, aspirin, mosquito repellent, and first aid kit. The belt from the fanny pack holds my canteens, pepper spray and 44 Magnum pistol if I'm in the back country of Alaska which has a large population of bears and wolves.

Now, let me elaborate on the contents of my pack that made my bear hunting adventure a story with the happy ending. As I mentioned, my little Bic cigarette lighter let me down in the field when soaked from torrential rains. As also mentioned, I carry the standard flint and steel type fire making outfit. A couple of scrapes on the flint and I produced fire with my hunting knife. Both flint and steel make beautiful sparks for days on end even when immersed in water for years. My Bic on the other hand, must dry out before it is of any use. To complement the flint, I also carry homemade "starter fuel" which I can easily ignite with my flint in any sort of weather (to include torrential rain and wind). The fuel is the key that allows me to start fires when others cannot. I prepare and store it using common household products like: 35mm film containers, a candle, cotton balls, Vaseline, a metal shoe polish container, and an old bicycle tire. Here's what you do.

Take the old bicycle tire and cut it into strips about one inch by four inches. Remove the top from the shoe polish container. Use the lid as a pan to melt some regular Vaseline (petroleum jelly). I use the shoe polish top since my spouse won't let me use her small sauté pans. You can improvise or wait till your spouse is out shopping or something. First, place some Vaseline into your pan and heat it over the candle until it turns clear. This will only take a few minutes. Then, take some cotton balls and dip them into the clarified Vaseline. They'll soak up the warm liquid like a sponge. You can drench them or just get them moist. I've found that the middle ground is about the best. Now, take about eight balls and place them into a film container. You don't need waterproof containers, however, they're light and don't take up much space. (You may immerse the soaked cotton balls in water immediately after dipping and they will light just as easily–if not better–than dry cotton balls. They will definitely burn longer.)

To use the balls, take one from the container and pull it apart (try to fluff it to twice the original size). Address a few sparks from your flint onto the ball and it will light. Each ball will give you approximately five minutes of flame. You can now build a little teepee as you would when starting a campfire. Now spray or rub a little mosquito repellent on your wet wood as an added incentive for it to burn. It encourages wood to burn since it is quite flammable. Please be careful and never spray it directly on the flames. Last, but, not least, here's where you use the bicycle tire. Once your teepee is afire, lay a strip of the bicycle inner tube over the top of the teepee. The rubber will burn hotter than the wood you have used on the fire. It allows you to add larger pieces sooner than the "old fashioned" way. Once added, the rubber also enables you to burn wet wood that became soaked the same time you did in the downpour.

Back to my story. Around 2:15 a.m., I heard the distinctive sound of an outboard motor coming up river. Within minutes I saw my hunting companions run from the boat, scramble up the bank and take up places around my toasty fire. They were cold, wet, and utterly miserable. All talked at once, explaining how the boat

continued on page 130

conked out in midstream while heading up river. The lone man piloting the boat used the anchor to pull himself to the other side of the river while drifting downstream. He tossed the anchor to one side of the boat then pulled it back in repeatedly. In time, he was able to maneuver across the river eventually ending up on the same side as our camp. Then he hiked upstream to the other boat we had there. Next, he began his trip upstream to pick up destitute hunters. Eventually my warm fire came into sight. Now we all gathered in the light of the fire to share our thoughts (and fears). No one else was able to get a fire going. Waterproof matches were easily broken by stiff and numb fingers. Bics wouldn't spark once wet. A Zippo ran out of fluid. Dry wood was unavailable... and of course, no one else remembered that mosquito repellent is usually quite flammable.

Since that fateful day, I'll never hunt or hike alone unless I have my survival pack with me. Take my advice, when you least expect it, the unexpected may become reality. It's then that you'll find yourself stuck in a bad dream you'll think may never end.

Leo Gonnering with barren ground caribou in Alaska

How Well Do You Know The Basics?

A quiz to test your hunting savvy

Being a responsible big game hunter requires that you know the basics of trailing and recovering big game animals. See how well you know the basics by answering the following questions:

1. After hitting a big game animal, how long should you wait before starting to trail it?
   A. Immediately; B. 10 minutes; C. One hour; D. 4 hours

2. If you run out of blood sign on the trail, you should:
   A. Start walking in ever-widening circles around the last sign.
   B. Start walking in a grid pattern using compass readings.
   C. Keep walking in the line that the last spotted blood signs were located.
   D. Check along the trail on which the animal first appeared.
   E. All of the above.

3. True or false: Heart shot animals may travel surprising distances and show little external bleeding.

4. True or false: If a deer is hit in the leg, you need to wait for at least one hour before trailing.

5. Blood that is frothy with bubbles indicates the animal was hit where?
   A. Liver or kidney
   B. Stomach
   C. Lung
   D. Neck
   E. Either C or D

6. Very dark blood may indicate the animal was hit where?
   A. Liver or kidney
   B. Stomach
   C. Lung
   D. Neck

7. When locating the animal and determining that it is dead the first job is to ——————— .

Answers are on page 191.

131

Fred Bear's Roast Ribs

Serves: 2 to 6
Prep Time: 2 hours

Ribs (Mountain sheep, mountain goat, moose, caribou or deer)

Cut two green forked stakes and two poles about four feet long. Make four S hooks from coat hangers or baling wire. Break the ribs with a hatchet or axe every 4 or 5 inches. Fasten two S hooks top and bottom.

In the meantime, start a fire after clearing away the leaves and other inflammables. If hardwood is available, it will take some time to burn to a bed of hot coals at which time you drive the forked stakes and hang the meat to roast. A good bed of hardwood coals should be sufficient to roast the ribs.

If your fuel is coniferous, the coals will not burn as long and wood must be added from time to time.

If you have aluminum foil, shape a rectangular pan to catch the drippings for basting although this is not a must.

Lift the pole from which the ribs are hung and turn from time to time. Turn them upside down occasionally also. To do this, the other pole is made fast to the bottom S hooks. Lift the ribs up by the top pole and, with the other hand, grasp the bottom pole. Turn them 180° and place back on the forked sticks. These turnings, both front to back and top to bottom, assure a uniformity of cooking and reverses the flow of juices to prevent drying out.

It will be ready to eat in about two hours, when the meat turns brown or when you can no longer stand the heavenly aroma.

"...where do ya want this moose meat?..."

★★★★★★★★★★★★★★★★★★

Doug and Jeff were in Wyoming scouting for elk when they saw a giant grizzly running their direction. Jeff whipped off his backpack, pulled off his boots and started putting on his running shoes. Doug said, "What are you doing, you can't outrun that angry bear." Jeff replied, "I don't have to outrun that bear, I just need to outrun you."

Did You Know?

One out of every 15 hunters in America today is a bowhunter. There are 15 million licensed hunters and more than 1,250,000 licensed bowhunters, according to the Wildlife Management Institute. Archery is now an official gold medal Olympic sport and in 1972 in Munich and again in the 1976 Montreal Olympics the United States won both the men's and women's gold medals.

Hunting Season

Roy M. Carson, Belleville, Pennsylvania

This poem came to the Club with the letter below:

My father died in September of 1990, and when I was going through his things, I found this poem he wrote years ago. I thought it could be of interest to you. Thank you.

Albert M. Carson, Belleville, Pennsylvania

The fall of the year is the best by score,
In November when the guns begin to roar.
That's the time that you love best,
So you go and put on your hunting vest.
And grab your gun and away you go,
Through rain, hail, sleet, or snow.
And every joke always seems funny,
When you go to look for mister bunny.
Sometimes there are three, four or five,
It makes you feel good to be alive.

Then comes the time to test your work,
When you go to hunt the foxy turk.
You set for hours and hours on end,
Till finally you spy a turkey hen.
You take a good aim and blast away,
But this does not seem your lucky day.
You take another as she sails along,
And you take another but the shot's too long.
You swear you'll get her some other day,
Because she was a big one that got away.

As you go slipping along the spur,
All at once you hear a funny whir.
As a grouse wings its way along,
Your gun roars out its mighty song.
The feathers fly, and the grouse comes down,
When you go over to look around.
You pick her up, and think just then,
"Why couldn't this have been that turkey hen."

Out along the spur, a little farther yet,
You see a chippie, go up a tree and set.
It's a great temptation for you or me,
When we see him set upon that tree.
Then it's time to hunt the old gray squirrel,
And you set for hours till it's so cold you curl.
Finally you see one out on a limb,

You pull up your gun and take a shot at him.
As the echo of the shot dies away,
Down on the ground the gray squirrel lay.

Then comes the month of December,
When all good sportsmen like to remember.
That it's time to go and try your luck,
And try and shoot yourself a buck.
There's many a gang goes to their camp,
And each gang has their story champ.
They set around their old camp fire,
And each man knows he is a liar.

The next day early and bright,
They're all up long before daylight.
The first drive each one is set,
To see which one a buck will get.
If they do not have any luck,
They drive another for their buck.
The one side waits upon their stand,
Each one has his gun in hand.
As the drive progresses along,
The standers can hear their merry song.

As the drive keeps coming out,
Suddenly one of the drivers shout.
"Look out there, look out ahead."
And soon someone is shooting lead.
The buck he springs, but it is too late,
And the doe ahead she knows his fate.
The buck falls upon the ground,
His head falls over, he makes no sound.
Then all the gang gathers around the kill,
And ask, "Who shot him, did you Bill?"
"Yes," said Bill, "He came on the run,
He came across here so I give him the gun."

They drove some more, and still some more,
Till finally a gun begins to roar.
A large buck goes flying through,
Another man opens up too.
Till five of the hunters were blasting away,
But the flying buck, he did not stay.
They hunt till the evening sun is low,
And towards their camp they finally go.
The season is over before they know,
And winter starts with ice and snow.
They must give up their quest for deer,
But they'll all be back again next year.

·THE GREAT· Whitetail Quiz

This section of The Great White-Tail Quiz (which started way back on page 18) has some real brain-busters for you. More questions are on pages 144-145.

63) Fawn does which are bred are usually bred:
A. Earlier than the adult does.
B. About the same time as the adult does.
C. Later than the adult does.

64) The majority of breeding takes place in a span of:
A. A few days.
B. One week.
C. Three weeks.

65) In general, whitetails weigh more:
A. In the northern part of their range.
B. In the southern part of their range.
C. Weights vary little regardless of geographical area.

66) The average deer hide weighs approximately:
A. Four to six pounds.
B. 10 to 12 pounds.
C. 15 to 20 pounds.

—R.STUBLER—

67) The most common method used by biologists to age deer in the field is to:
A. Measure the antlers.
B. Weigh the deer.
C. Examine tooth wear.

68) A whitetail's top running speed is about:
A. 35 to 40 miles per hour.
B. 45 to 50 miles per hour.
D. 60 to 65 miles per hour.

69) Whitetails can swim at speeds of about:
A. Five miles per hour.
B. Nine miles per hour.
C. 13 miles per hour.

70) The tail of a whitetail is:
A. Shorter than that of a mule deer.
B. Longer than that of a mule deer.

71) Most antler damage occurs:
A. While the bucks are in velvet.
B. As a result of buck fights.
C. While bucks rub saplings.

72) Whitetails have _____ sets of external glands.
A. Two
B. Four
C. Six

73) The largest of the whitetail's external glands is the:
A. Preorbital gland.
B. Interdigital gland.
C. Tarsal gland.

74) An adult deer has:
A. 24 teeth.
B. 32 teeth.
C. 38 teeth.

75) In the wild, does generally live:
A. Shorter lives than bucks.
B. Longer lives than bucks.
C. About the same length of time as bucks.

Answers are on page 185.

National Park Stories

A camper at Long Pine Key in Everglades National Park decided to take a dip in the lake with her dog despite signs saying "No Swimming–Danger–Alligators." She swam to an island about 75 yards from the shore, then saw some alligators and refused to swim back. "Didn't you see the signs?" asked the ranger who retrieved her in a canoe. "Sure," she said, "but I didn't think they applied to me."

In May of 1994, Tony Moore, 43, of Marietta, Georgia, was gored and seriously injured by a large male bison in Yellowstone, next to the Lake Hotel. Moore and a friend had approached to within 15 feet of the bison to have their pictures taken. While they were standing with their backs to the animal, it charged. Moore's companion escaped, but Moore received a severe puncture wound in his right thigh and was taken by ambulance to a hospital in Jackson for treatment.

In 1994, a woman visiting from the Bay Area embarked on a solo hike to the summit of El Capitan in Yosemite. When she became lost and saw a storm brewing, she called 911 from her cellular phone and asked to be rescued. A helicopter found her barely off the trail and one-fourth to one-half a mile from the top of El Cap. When the 'copter lifted off and the woman saw how close she was to her summit goal, she asked the crew to set her down on top. When the crew declined, she threatened to sue them for kidnapping.

A woman, appearing rather distraught, came to the visitor center at Redwood National Park in California to report that she had seen several Irish setters lying along the edge of the highway and she feared they were dead or injured. Rangers explained to her that these were pieces of redwood bark that had fallen off the logging trucks.

Darryl Stone, now superintendent at Jefferson National Expansion Memorial in St. Louis, remembered working the entrance station at Yosemite when a woman drove up and aksed, "Which way are the geysers?" Ranger Stone directed her to continue 1,000 miles further to Yellowstone and told her there were no geysers at Yosemite. "Yes, there are," she said. "I have a friend who saw them." Stone and the woman went round and round several times before she left, insisting that there were geysers at Yosemite. Later she wrote a letter to the chief ranger complaining that Stone had refused to provide her with the information she wanted.

When an elderly couple stopped to film some bears at Dunraven Pass in Yellowstone, a young bear crawled into their car searching for food. Unable to make the bear leave, the exasperated (but well-dressed) couple drove about 17 miles to the ranger station at Canyon Village with the bear in the back seat. When the husband got out to report the incident, the bear hopped over into the front seat so that investigating rangers found the woman in the passenger seat and the bear behind the wheel.

Field Care Of Your Trophy Animal

Wayne Thomas, Life Member and
Owner of Thomas Taxidermy,
Pittsburgh, Pennsylvania

NAHC Member's Story

I am a Life Member of the NAHC, and a licensed taxider-mist. I talk to as many people as I can at sportsmen's shows, hunter safety courses, sportsmen's clubs, etc. on the proper handling of game and think these tips, if more peo-ple were aware of them, would help other sportsmen and taxidermists. A lot of them are commonsense type tips, but in the heat of excitement over taking a trophy animal, common sense is thrown to the wind.

Do not hang big game from a rope by the neck. This breaks hair and could cause a rope burn effect on the finished mount.

When dragging game, try to keep the head and shoulders off the ground to keep from pulling out hair and causing bald spots.

Wipe excess blood from the hair on game intended to be mounted – especially white hair. Some big game hair is hollow and if the blood penetrates and becomes trapped inside the hair, it may not be able to be removed.

If you must dispatch a big game animal that is not yet dead, **do not** cut the throat and **do not** shoot it in the head or neck. Make sure the animal is not on a rock or hard surface and no one is in the line of fire. Stand back and shoot the animal once behind the front shoulder through the lungs. The animal will die in a matter of seconds.

Always allow any animal to cool before placing it in any type of container. **Do not** enclose an animal in a tightly closed plastic bag. Plastic will not allow any air to circu-late. If the animal is not completely cooled down, bacteria will start to form and hair slippage or meat spoilage may occur. Use a burlap or paper bag to allow circulation. If plastic must be used, always make sure the animal is completely cooled down and leave the top of the bag open, not tied in a knot. ••••

Just Don't Hunt From Your Car

The riskiest part of a hunting trip in New York state is the drive. A hunter is 21 times more likely to be injured while driving than while hunting.

According to the State Department of Environmental Conservation, about 750,000 sportsmen hunt in New York each year with less than 1 accident for each 10,000 participants.

New York hunters annually make about 10 million hunting trips traveling an average of 6 miles resulting in about 1,600 injuries on the road compared With only about 75 hunting accidents.

Maybe the Department of Motor Vehicles should take a lesson from the New York Sportsman Education program which requires all new hunters to take at least 10 hours of special training to qualify for a hunting license.

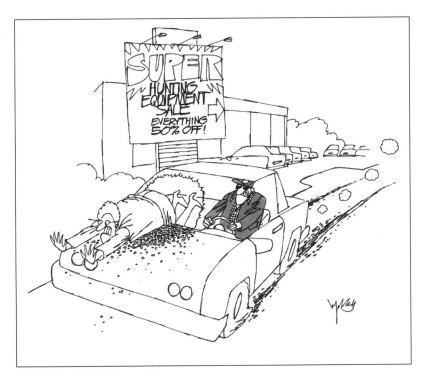

Can you name the

27

North American big game animals that comprise the legendary

Super Slam ?

@ANDERSON...

1. _____
2. _____
3. _____
4. _____
5. _____
6. _____
7. _____
8. _____
9. _____
10. _____
11. _____
12. _____
13. _____
14. _____
15. _____
16. _____
17. _____
18. _____
19. _____
20. _____
21. _____
22. _____
23. _____
24. _____
25. _____
26. _____
27. _____

Answers are on page 191.

For the hunter is the joy of the horse well ridden and the rifle well held; for him the long days of toil and hardship, resolutely endured, and crowned at the end with triumph. In after-years there shall come forever to his mind the memory of endless prairies shimmering in the bright sun; of vast snow-clad wastes lying desolate under gray skies; of the melancholy marshes; of the rush of mighty rivers; of the breath of the evergreen forest in summer; of the crooning of ice-armored pines at the touch of the winds of winter; of cataracts roaring between hoary mountain passes; of all the innumerable sights and sounds of the wilderness; of its immensity and mystery; and of the silences that brood in its still depth.

Theodore Roosevelt

There's More Now
Than Ever Before

In 1887, there were no whitetail deer left in Pennsylvania. By 1900 there were only 500,000 deer left in all of the United States.

Elk had dwindled from 10 million animals to less than 50,000 in scattered pockets in several western states.

By 1908 there were less than 25,000 pronghorn antelope in North America.

Between 1885 and 1910, our original big game supplies had faded by more than 80 percent!

As a result of proper game management initiated by president Teddy Roosevelt, who was a member of the Boone & Crockett Club, and other far-sighted men, those 50,000 elk have now grown to approximately 1 million.

Those 25,000 antelope back in 1908 are nothing compared to the more than 1 million presently roaming the western ranges.

Perhaps most dramatically, that small group of 500,000 deer has grown to more than 20 million whitetails and another 1,500,000 mule deer.

During the last two decades the deer population in the South has increased by 800 percent, and Alabama allows one deer per day during the season because the herd exceeds the habitat's carrying capacity.

And since 1920, deer populations in the national forests have increased five-fold, according to the Department of the Interior's Bureau of Sport Fisheries and Wildlife.

Y ou're almost at the end of this informative quiz which started on page 18. After you've finished this section, turn to page 164 for the final part!

76) Deer in captivity have lived as long as:
A. 16½ years.
B. 19½ years.
C. 24½ years.

77) Possibly the heaviest buck fawn on record was shot in Illinois in 1966. The buck fawn weighed (live weight):
A. 132 pounds.
B. 176 pounds.
C. 218 pounds.

78) During the breeding season, mature bucks may lose as much as _____ of their body weight.
A. 20 to 25 percent.
B. 35 to 40 percent.
C. 45 to 50 percent.

79) Whitetails deposit about _____ pellet groups per day.
A. Seven; B. 10; C. 13.

80) The sole purpose of scrapes is to aid bucks in locating does during the breeding season.
A. True; B. False.

81) The sole purpose of rubs is to serve as a means for bucks to strengthen their neck muscles.
A. True; B. False.

82) The throat of a dead deer must be slit to allow the blood to drain.
A. True; B. False.

83) Musk glands will not taint the venison of a dead deer.
A. True; B. False.

84) A whitetail's winter coat provides such excellent insulation that snow will not be melted where a deer beds down.
A. True;   B. False.

85) Buck fights are more violent than sparring matches.
A. True;   B. False.

86) Buck fights occur more frequently than sparring matches.
A. True;   B. False.

87) Buck fights frequently result in serious injury to one or both of the combatants.
A. True;   B. False.

Answers are on page 185.

Scout As Late As Possible

Your more serious scouting should be as close to opening day as possible. Deer have a way of changing habits just before the hunting season opens. They begin switching from late summer to fall foods. Colder days mean that bedding areas will change. The rut is coming on and the bucks are becoming restless and covering more ground. The later you scout, the more accurate and up-to-date your findings will be, increasing your chances of being in the right place at the right time on opening morning.

TOMASIC

"Baker 6 to Alpha 5: Bogie in Sector Omega 9!"

Roland The Hunter

Adam Wendelschafer, Cleveland, MN

As I sat in my blind on a southern Minnesota lake on the opening morning of duck season I looked across the lake to see a boat headed right for me. I leaned to my hunting buddy and asked, "That couldn't be him, could it?" It was. Across the lake with everything including the kitchen sink came Roland Wells with his son. They parked in the weeds some 200 yards away and we didn't hear from them until 45 minutes into the season.

"Help! Help!" came shouts from his son after some shots were fired at passing mallards. We rushed to them to find they had tipped their fully loaded boat when they took their first shots. After hours of searching for all their gear and uprighting their boat our opening day was over, but that didn't surprise me because good ole' Roland had a knack for making things interesting.

"Hey Roland, that new goose call really works!"

This was the same Roland who after he decided his Saab was a death trap on the highway, would park it at deer camp and use it as a deer puller. That worked until he had to cross a stream and got stuck deep. With four guys pushing and a Chevy Blazer pulling we got him out only to watch him drive it up on a stump and almost roll it. That was the end of that.

This was also the same Roland who decided to take the ice scraper from his car and bring it into his deer stand. Just after it got light he proceeded to scrape, and I mean scraaaaaaaape, his floor. Now you might not think too much of this but in a silent, snow covered woods, that noise can be heard for miles. We could actually see the deer rolling around in the snow laughing at him.

Now with Roland you never quite know what would happen, but one thing you could count on is that something always would. I guess that's always why I enjoyed hunting with him.

Weigh Your Deer With A Dollar

You can weigh your deer with a dollar bill. That's right, George, Abe and the more costly greenbacks all work with an amazing degree of accuracy.

Borrowing this technique from the cattle industry and verifying it with university wildlife researchers, experts have found this quick way to weigh your trophy.

Carry along a piece of string, shoelace or drag rope to wrap around the deer's chest behind the front legs. Note the spot on the string that shows its girth, or distance around the deer. Pull out a dollar bill from your wallet and notice that it is always six inches long. Use that to measure the length of the string to the girth mark.

Just compare that number of inches to the chart below, which you can rip out and carry in your wallet, and you will be able to read across to your deer's live weight, dressed weight and edible meat predictions.

For you doubting Thomases, after you've tried this method, verify its accuracy at a certified scale.

GIRTH	LIVE WEIGHT	DRESSED	EDIBLE MEAT
20″	49 lb.	32 lb.	23 lb.
22″	56 lb.	38 lb.	26 lb.
24″	65 lb.	45 lb.	30 lb.
26″	74 lb.	53 lb.	34 lb.
28″	85 lb.	62 lb.	38 lb.
30″	97 lb.	73 lb.	44 lb.
32″	111 lb.	85 lb.	50 lb.
34″	127 lb.	99 lb.	57 lb.
36″	145 lb.	114 lb.	65 lb.
38″	166 lb.	132 lb.	74 lb.
40″	191 lb.	153 lb.	85 lb.
42″	218 lb.	177 lb.	97 lb.
44″	250 lb.	204 lb.	110 lb.
46″	286 lb.	234 lb.	126 lb.

Animal Rights Sandwiches

Serves: 1
Prep Time: 5 minutes

2 rabbits
2 squirrels
2 artichokes
1 head of lettuce
  Bread
  Butter

Let the rabbits and squirrels go free. Don't cut the heart out of the artichoke because it has rights just like humans. Leave the head of lettuce alone. You can butter the bread and eat that.

Joe Sarcasm
Mentillee, Illinois

To make dragging go as smoothly as possible when trying to get your deer out of the woods, bring the forelegs up and tie them inside of the antlers to stream-line the animal.

A light rope or nylon cord tied around the neck just below the head works well, especially if the other end is tied to a strong stick to distribute the weight among avail-able hands. This works ideally for two hunters dragging a single deer.

"If old **Wally** here knows he's goin' huntin' everything lets loose..."

The Deer Woods Word Search

```
A  W  L  L  S  D  S  G  N  I  P  P  O  R  D
H  E  O  T  S  U  A  T  B  I  G  G  A  M  E
S  A  S  N  O  S  A  E  S  R  I  A  H  H  O
U  T  B  U  C  K  S  T  E  K  C  I  H  T  L
D  H  B  E  P  L  A  N  T  L  E  R  S  N  A
N  E  N  E  F  D  T  R  E  V  O  L  C  G  A
N  R  R  D  A  E  C  R  A  R  E  S  F  I  D
U  L  U  D  C  E  E  L  A  Y  T  E  A  S  A
K  B  T  E  O  N  S  D  I  I  F  P  A  N  W
R  A  E  N  R  E  I  W  S  M  L  A  A  L  N
U  F  I  D  N  S  H  K  O  I  T  R  I  T  S
B  A  H  O  S  U  C  L  D  R  B  C  E  F  O
S  W  L  L  O  A  G  O  O  D  B  S  L  U  C
K  N  H  A  R  V  E  A  S  S  C  E  N  T  S
A  J  B  T  S  T  O  L  D  O  O  W  C  E  W
```

ACORNS	DROPPINGS	SCRAPES
ANTLERS	DUSK	SEASONS
BED	FAWN	SIGN
BIGGAME	FEED	THICKETS
BROWSE	HAIR	TRACKS
BUCK	RUBS	TRAIL
CLOVER	RUT	WEATHER
DAWN	SCENTS	WOODLOTS
DOE		

Answers are on page 186.

149

The Oldest Whitetail In The Woods

H. John Rice

I was already awake when the alarm sounded at 3:30 a.m. It was November 10th, the first day of Kentucky's split whitetail hunting season. The second season was to follow in December.

David, my 19-year-old son, was up too, and we hurriedly dressed while the coffee was brewing. After a quick breakfast, we loaded the pickup with our guns and equipment and headed for the hunting area we had selected, approximately 18 miles away.

If our 14-pointer was to be where we were almost certain he would be at daybreak, we had to keep the wind from him to us. So we zippered up our jackets, shouldered our rifles and headed out on foot to one of three possible positions.

We walked softly through an open field by way of another farm, and circled back to the timber's edge, arriving 45 minutes before the break of dawn, as planned.

We decided after arriving at our stand under a large red cedar tree, to stay together instead of separating. The wind was shifting, and we figured it was better to stay put instead of spreading our scent all over the place. It later proved to be a very wise decision.

This was the third year David and I, as well as many other hunters, had been after this deer. Two years before we had given up, and I shot a small eight-point buck some 500 yards from where we were now standing. When we had finished field dressing it and turned to get some poles to carry him with, we spotted our 14-point buck staring at us 150 yards away. We made the mistake of moving too quickly for our guns, which were leaning against some nearby trees. He was gone in a flash, disappearing over a ridge.

While scouting during the fall, I had watched this 14-point buck go into the large depressed area we were watching and bed down early after feeding on the soybeans. He did, however, bed down a few times in the large timber or broomsedge near where we were standing. We felt certain however on this cold damp day he would go to the large depressed area.

Dawn arrived and it was light enough that we could see the sloping terrain in the valley below. We could not see a deer feeding in the soybean field or even so much as hear one, so we waited. At 6:30 a.m., someone fired from the small patch of large timber below to the right. He fired again; then a third time. Four hundred yards away, over a fence to the west, leaped a big 10-point buck and three does that we knew had run with the 14-pointer at times. David whispered that guy had blown it for us. I whispered, "No, that is not the 14-pointer. Watch the large depressed area."

Almost instantly, David said, "I see movement in the depressed area!" Then I saw it. Behind the first action was a second movement. We spotted a doe coming toward us; a buck was behind her.

"I can't tell how big he is," David whispered. "He's hunched behind the doe, but he's coming this way." I also could not tell what size buck he was.

The doe and buck came toward us. The doe was still in the lead as they passed a large poplar tree in the middle of the field. They stopped on the edge of the soybean acreage.

The buck was behind the poplar slowly raising his head to look over the large limbs. We stood motionless.

His white throat was distinctly visible as he stood still. His silhouette was vaguely visible to us. He managed to obscure his antlers behind the tree and other growth.

The doe, looking back, finally decided to take the center trail to the heavy timber in which we were standing. We

continued on page 152

151

felt certain the buck would follow. The buck hesitated, then followed her.

When he came out from behind the tree, I spotted his rack. It was so wide and heavy that it had to be the 14-pointer. I whispered softly to David, and to myself, "Keep it cool. Keep it cool."

I began leading the buck with my Ruger M77 chambered in .280 Remington. When the crosshairs of my Bushnell scope seemed right, I sent the 125-grain Core-Lokt on its way.

The buck just stopped and looked back. The doe broke into a run. David quickly centered him in his sights and fired just as the buck took off. He was really moving when I found him in the scope again. I fired when the crosshairs passed his right shoulder. He dropped as the echo of my shot died away. We could see his antlers above the broomsedge 205 yards away.

D avid and I ran to him. His antlers were nontypical but his rack was beautiful. He had 16 points over an inch long instead of 14. 1 was so nervous I just could not tag him right then. I just sat down. It had been a long time since I had a seizure of buck fever like this.

We later discovered that David had hit the buck through the outer edge of the liver.

We checked him in at the official check station after we had field dressed him. Without his heart and liver he weighed 214 pounds. His rack was the attraction of the day. The local television station even put him on the sports show several times.

The taxidermist who mounted him told me that when he had finished mounting him and placed him on the wall of his antique shop, 26 people were lined up outside before opening time the next morning to view him.

The deer's inside right ear has a notch in it. It is believed that this is the buck that was trapped with five does at Mammoth Cave National Park and released on the very farm on which we were hunting. The notch is believed to be the result of the lost ear tag.

David's boss told my son that he was the one who hauled the buck and five does to this farm and released them for the local sportsman's club 15 years ago.

A nearby neighbor told me that he had seen this buck for the past 11 years. This is almost unbelievable, as this buck's meat was as tender and succulent as any whitetail I have ever eaten.

Even though I fired the fatal shot, David's assistance made this the most memorable hunt I have ever been on.

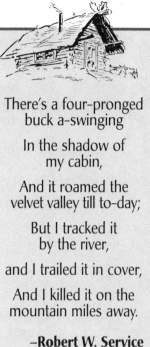

There's a four-pronged buck a-swinging

In the shadow of my cabin,

And it roamed the velvet valley till to-day;

But I tracked it by the river,

and I trailed it in cover,

And I killed it on the mountain miles away.

–Robert W. Service
The Rhyme of the Remittance Man

"This one was in rut."

Rebel For Sale

A man is looking through the paper and sees an ad that says "Retriever for sale, best duck and goose dog you'll find anywhere. It's a steal, only $100.00." He calls the number and the owner of the dog invites the man to go duck hunting with him, so he can see how good the dog is.

They go to the lake and are sitting in a duck blind. A flock of ducks flies over and they knock one down, about 50 yards from the blind. The dog owner says to the dog, "Fetch, Rebel!"

The dog runs across the top of the water, grabs the duck and runs on top of the water, back to the blind, barely getting his feet wet.

The dog owner says, "There, have you ever seen any dog that could do that?"

The man says,"I don't want him."

The dog owner says, "Why not? You must be nuts!"

The man says, "That dog can't swim!"

—Chuck Tudor, Mikado, Michigan

"I can tell this story just fine by myself, 'Man's-Best-Friend'!"

More National Park Stories

A visitor to Glacier National Park in Montana lost his car keys while attempting to lure a ground squirrel by dangling the keys out in front of the critter. The squirrel grabbed the keys and ran down a hole with them. The keys were never retrieved, a ranger cited the man for harassment of wildlife, and a locksmith was called to make new car keys.

+ +

Each year visitors to Petrified Forest National Park in Arizona pocket an estimated 12 tons of petrified wood to take home (despite numerous warnings not to take the wood and the fact that this criminal violation carries a minimum fine of $275). Some years back, several female foreign visitors, clad only in bikinis, were observed hiding wood in their garments. Another time, rangers received a report that a man had put a large piece of wood in his car. Upon searching his vehicle, they found a 40-pound piece of petrified wood in his trunk. According to rangers, this visitor said he didn't know how it got there. "My four-year-old son must have put it there," the man said.

● ●

A group of European visitors came to the Wawona ranger station in Yosemite National Park and said, "Our car is parked at the trail head and it's been blown up by terrorists." Though rangers expressed some doubt, the visitors insisted that a bomb had exploded in their car and that they could see powder residue from the explosives. Investigating rangers indeed found that a door had been torn off and a powder-like substance — pancake flour — was strewn about the car. "They were quite embarrassed when we showed them the bear prints, " the ranger said.

< > < > < > < > < > < > < > < > < > < > < > < > < > < > < >

The Hunt

ACROSS
1. Rut
7. Cow sound
9. Animal skin
10. Knife handle material
11. Heavy load (abbr.)
14. Six point bull elk
16. Like a fox
17. Where bears go in winter
20. Stone-age hunting axe
21. Hunter's headgear
22. Type of scope for hunters
25. One Abe Lincoln
26. Right-angle structure
27. Canada, snow, speck etc.
28. Bull elk playgrounds
32. Our country (abbr.)
34. Vanish without a _____
36. First name in bow records
38. Not down
40. Arched part of foot

41. Exclamation
42. Government environ-
    mental agency (abbr.)
43. Type of sheep
45. Broken tree stump
47. Used in life vests
48. Shoo!
49. Type of tree
50. Wilderness transportation
51. Where you keep trophies
52. Puma, bobcat, lynx etc.

DOWN
2. They play on the range
3. Works for outfitter
4. Type of tree
5. Exclamation
6. Type of elk call
7. Who's a good hunter?
8. Take you hunting for a fee
12. Small word
13. Large bear

15. Cowboy's exclamation
18. Type of grouse
19. Scents for hunting deer
22. Looking for game
23. Sitting ___ stand
24. Golden calf was one
28. Used to be
29. Sheltered side of hill
30. Indian name for elk
31. Type of salmon
33. To eat (colloquial)
35. Medical personnel
37. Recreational areas
39. Hooded jackets
44. Great group of dedicated
    hunters (abbr.)
45. Term of respect
46. Needed for outboard
48. Leave or depart
49. Small word

Answers on page 188.

156

Good Dogs
Bill Miller

Staff Story

W ho can look into the eyes of a springer spaniel;
watch the playful antics of a retriever pup; sense
the excitement in the quivering muscles of a
locked-up pointer or setter and still not believe that the
dog has a soul? Could anyone who has ever loved a canine
argue that a faithful bird dog is not entitled to the same
revelations at death that we attribute to the human spirit?

If in human death there is a revelation that answers all
the questions accrued during a lifetime, then a faithful
hunting dog deserves as much. None of us will ever know
until we get there whether such a phenomenon occurs, but
I believe as surely as I believe in opening day, that when an
aged springer named Bingo died, a long-sought answer was
revealed to him.

I t was a snowy morning in Wisconsin's early March
when Ted Miller came in from the barn with the report
for his family that Bingo, the oldest dog in their kennel,
seemed to be resting better. Perhaps his long bout with
pneumonia was nearly over.

Those two had spent a lot of time together during the
last 14 years. Verbal commands were hardly necessary for
Ted to let the dog know what he wanted, and Ted could
usually understand what the dog was trying to tell him. In
fact, the last two seasons the dog had hunted he was totally
deaf, he just got used to stopping and looking around for
occasional hand signals.

This morning Ted read his dog's disposition correctly.
The end of the dog's suffering was near, but not in the way
he was hoping for.

On his way out the door to work, Ted told his wife to
keep the horses inside until the weather broke or go down
to the barn at noon and throw them a little hay if the
storm was still blowing too hard to put them outside.
Bingo would need his dose of medicine, too.

continued on page 158

Good Dogs *continued from page 157*

Ted said he would call from work around 1:00 or so to see if everything was going ok. It was still snowing hard when Ted stopped at the barn on his way out of the driveway. He got out of the pickup and went in to pull the grain pans from the horses' stalls and run his hand over Bingo's graying head. Then he drove on to town.

In the barn, the snow sifted in around the edges of the doors and built drifts—miniatures of those piling up outside. Steam rose from the freshly thawed and refilled water buckets in each box stall and kennel run. Sparrows dropped from roosts in the rafters to eat spilled grain next to the storage barrels.

As is often the case during a heavy snowfall, it was quiet in the stable. The straw in the stall rustled when a quarter horse shifted its weight. Now and then one of the dogs would yawn and whine. The only constant sound was Bingo's raspy breath from the warm corner between two box stalls.

Under ordinary circumstances all of the dogs were confined to kennels unless under supervision, but Bingo's illness was not an ordinary circumstance. Nor was he an ordinary dog.

To look at him now, it might have been difficult to imagine that this wheezing, sickly, deaf, gray-muzzled dog lying in a bed of shavings was the same pup who put veteran dogs to shame before he was two years old. The same die-hard hunter who would always feign making game when the pickup was in sight at the end of the day. The same Binghampton Hunter III who doubled as an obedience dog and tacked the initials C.D. (Companion Dog) onto his already formidable title.

This deathbed was a long, long way from the day when Bingo put a sparkle of pride in Ted's eyes as the dog made his first double retrieve on a pair of big, red-legged Canadian mallards. That first season was the kickoff to an enviable career. There were no field trial trophies, not even among Bingo's offspring. Fact is, Ted never ran him in a field trial, never even broke him to shot. But for the "back 40" type of hunting that Ted and Bingo did, they suited each other well.

Only the loss of a single rooster pheasant marred their hunting memories. It happened during the dog's third season.

They were hunting on the farm of a friend along the Onion River.  Bingo rousted a big, longtailed rooster from a clump of dogwood in the frozen swamp along the fast-flowing river. The bird banked left just as it took the charge of sixes sent on its way by Ted's 12-gauge. Feathers flew, the bird crumpled momentarily, then set its wings in a glide that took it out of sight around a small rise upstream. Ted hollered, "Dead bird!" though it wasn't necessary. Bingo was already rounding the base of the hill.

By the time Ted got there, the snow in a huge area was scattered with the dog's tracks as it quartered back and forth searching for the rooster's scent. Ted believed the bird had to be dead when it hit the ground.

Though they looked for an hour and hunted through that same area twice more during the afternoon, they never picked up that pheasant. Ted was sure that the bird was headed away from the river when he last saw it set in its glide.

What surely seemed like tougher assignments presented themselves in following seasons, but Bingo never faltered. He always found birds where bracemates failed. The dog's last season afield, some three years before this gray day in March was, likewise, without failure. It was a very good year.

continued on page 160

Good Dogs continued from page 159

The DNR had planted birds throughout the season in a small public hunting area very near the Miller farm, and hunting was very good. Ted and Bingo probably had chances at more than their fair share of birds during the quick hikes after work, and during the week of vacation Ted always saved for pre-winter chores and for hunting with the old dog. They never took more than their legal limit, but they hunted most every day. Ted figured that a deaf dog in his last season deserved that kind of indulgence. The birds weren't the long-spurred natives of the dog and master's youth, but they were fun just the same.

Even at the dog's slowed pace during the last season, there was some of that rough-and-ready, take-it-as-it-comes spirit left in him; the spirit which would spawn those sorrowful looks when he was called to kennel at day's end. That was the only time he would pretend not to know what Ted wanted of him.

But this morning that spirit was ebbing. The dog had put on a show for his master, but now stiff joints and aching muscles took time to react. With an effort, Bingo finally got to his feet and walked to a post in the center of the stable to lift his leg. A fresh scar from the removal of a tumor would have been evident had anyone been there to see it.

The dog went over to sniff his water bucket, but it was still warm. He went to a snow drift inside the door and bolted a couple mouthfuls. It helped cool his fever.

Back in his corner, head between his paws, Bingo's brown eyes began to glaze, only to clear for a moment. It was as though he finally understood the answer to a question that plagued him and his master for years.

He rose to his feet, went to the southeast comer of the stable and laid down again. Then his eyes closed for good. At noon, Ted's wife found Bingo's body stiff and cold.

When the telephone rang at 1:00 or so, she knew she couldn't tell him about the dog. It was better he found out for himself. Conversation strained, but she didn't think he knew.

Ted found Bingo when he went to exercise the rest of the dogs and feed the horses. The other chores were cast aside until what had to be done was done.

In a few minutes, sled tracks led away from the barn,

across a hay field, to the top of a small knoll where the family had planted some pine and spruce. The pick axe and shovel were missing from their pegs in the workshop.

More than an hour later, the last of the dirt packed back into place, Ted leaned his weight on the shovel handle and rested from the exertion of cutting down through several feet of frosted ground. His son had joined him moments before, sent by his mother to tell his father to come in for supper.

The young boy looked at his dad's face. The sparsely falling flakes landed on his dad's cheeks, then melted and trickled through his whiskers. To his son, the drops looked like they might be tears, but his dad would never cry.

The two turned and walked back to the house, towing the empty sled behind. They talked about life and about training dogs.

A few miles to the southeast of the fresh grave, the current of the Onion River piled more silt on the bleached bones of a rooster pheasant lost seasons before.

Reprinted from March/April '87 **North American Hunter**

"Just once more, Fred, and I think he will have the hang of it."

What Do You Call A Bunch Of ...

...deer, a herd.

...ducks, a flock.

...turkeys, a rafter.

...geese, a gaggle.

...lions, a pride.

...elk, a gang.

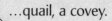

...fox, a skulk.

...doves, a dule.

...quail, a covey.

...dedicated
hunters,
the NAHC.

—R. STUBLER—

"I missed him six times before I bagged him."

The Beast
In The Forest
Teri Glover

I started deer hunting three years ago. My boyfriend brought me up to his uncle's farm, where he and six other guys hunt every year. I sat with my boyfriend the year before and he taught me the ropes, so the next year I was to brave it alone.

The guys knew I was hesitant about sitting alone, and they weren't hesitant in feeding my fear. They began to tell me stories about bobcats, wolves and bears, each story more wild than the last. I sifted through the most outlandish ones, but the overall picture left in my head was that the forest was filled with beasts that were going to come and get me.

Opening day I went and sat on my bale of hay tucked within some trees, for I was too scared to sit in a deer stand. I sat there quiet as a mouse, when all of a sudden I heard a snort behind me. I froze. I heard another one, and another one — they were loud! I was convinced it was a wild bear. I didn't breathe. He was so close it sounded like he was sitting right on my lap. I was too petrified to turn and look at him. Then he — whatever he was — must have left.

When it was time to go in I tripped through the snow back to the farm. I told the guys my horror story and they started to laugh. They told me that snorting was probably a buck visiting the scrape located behind my stand. Late afternoon when I returned to my bale I took a look, and sure enough, there was a large scrape beneath a tree! I never head that buck again all weekend.

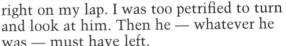

Finding Comfort

For more comfortable sitting in your climbing treestand, always try to find a tree that leans slightly back from the direction you want to face.

H ere it is—the last part of our Great White-Tail Quiz that started on page 18. You'll find the answers, and scoring information, on page 185.

88) Acorns are a highly nutritional deer food.
A. True; B. False.

89) White cedar is an excellent winter deer food.
A. True; B. False.

90) Hemlock is a poor quality winter deer food.
A. True; B. False.

91) Oak browse is as nutritional as acorns.
A. True; B. False.

92) Does generally enter winter in better shape than bucks.
A. True; B. False.

93) Spike bucks will eventually grow trophy racks if they live long enough.
A. True; B. False.

94) Whitetails decrease their daily intake of food in the winter even when food supplies are abundant.
A. True; B. False.

95) Does become noticeably more active during the breeding season.
A. True; B. False.

96) Antlered does are not capable of bearing fawns.
A. True; B. False.

97) Deer predators never prey on healthy animals.
A. True; B. False.

Answers are on page 185.

©ANDERSON···

Memories of the "Mertmobile"

Jeff Boehler

Hunting just wouldn't be the same without the hunting vehicle. Growing up in North Dakota I spent countless hours with my dad in the truck looking for one type of game bird or another. Some of my fondest memories are of those dark mornings on the way to the duck slough, the late mornings in the warm truck after a snowy goose hunt, and the long evenings driving west for sharptails.

Occasionally a hunting vehicle takes on a personality of its own, which is the case with the "Mertmobile." This giant '79 Ford extended cab pickup with over 287,000 (we're not exactly sure when the odometer quit working) hard miles is fondly named after my father-in-law and hunting partner Leland "Mert" Larson. I suppose if you log that many miles on any vehicle you're likely to acquire some stories, but the fact that

the Mertmobile always got us there and back is a testament to its manufacturer as well as its driver.

I'm pretty sure there was a time when the truck was new, and just when its decline started is difficult to say. It might have been when our friend Dave hopped in the passenger side and put his foot through the floorboard all the way up to his knee. Or it could have been when Joe (another son-in-law) was backing up in the woods for a load of freshly cut wood and a tree took off the driver side mirror. He readjusted the truck, backed up again and promptly removed the mirror on the passenger side.

The Mertmobile has helped me meet people I otherwise wouldn't know. One wet year we befriended a couple of generous farmers and their tractors up by the woods after becoming stuck on a few occasions. We also got to know a kind resort owner on the lake during a ride home after running out of gas on an ice fishing outing (the gas gauge didn't work then either).

I've also received a few auto maintenance lessons thanks to Mert and his truck. When the rear shaft disconnected on the way to the duck slough, the parts were simply removed, the truck was put in front wheel drive, and off we went. When the brakes went out on a goose hunting trip, Mert crawled under the truck, pinched a brake line with a vise grip behind the front wheels, and we continued hunting. When there was a short in the headlight switch and the lights would go out every few miles on the back roads to our slough, Mert would just slow down and keep pulling the switch until they popped back on. No sense in letting a few minor car problems ruin a good day's hunting.

There have been improvements made over the years. The box was held together for years by an increasing number of elastic cords, but that was remedied when Ole (another friend) left the truck idling in reverse rather than neutral. It backed into the side of a building which stood the rusty old box straight on its end. It now sports a new wooden box built with 2X4s and wood screws...do you remember the Clampett's truck on "The Beverly Hillbillies"?

I will always cherish the hours I spent in that truck with Mert riding to and from the field, the woods and the slough. The Mertmobile is now serving a cushy retirement in a garage, only to be used for plowing snow during our Minnesota winters. It has been replaced by an old Dodge that was purchased for $1...but that's another story.

Photo at left:
Official Member
Mert Larson with
Wyoming antelope

My Deer Hunt

Neil A. Goldade

NAHC Member's Story

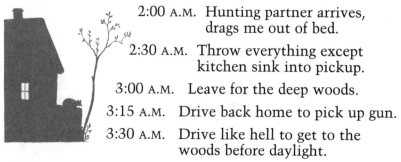

1:00 A.M.   Alarm clock rings.

2:00 A.M.   Hunting partner arrives, drags me out of bed.

2:30 A.M.   Throw everything except kitchen sink into pickup.

3:00 A.M.   Leave for the deep woods.

3:15 A.M.   Drive back home to pick up gun.

3:30 A.M.   Drive like hell to get to the woods before daylight.

4:00 A.M.   Set up camp. Forgot the damn tent.

4:30 A.M.   Head for the woods.

6:05 A.M.   See eight deer.

6:06 A.M.   Take aim and squeeze trigger.

6:07 A.M.   CLICK.

6:08 A.M.   Load gun while watching deer go over hill.

8:00 A.M.   Head back to camp.

9:00 A.M.   Still looking for camp.

10:00 A.M.   I realize I don't know where camp is.

Noon   Fire my gun for help. Eat wild berries.

12:15 P.M.   Run out of bullets. Eight deer come back.

12:20 P.M.   Strange feeling in my stomach.

12:30 P.M.   Realize I ate poison berries.

12:45 P.M.   Rescued.

12:55 P.M.   Rushed to hospital to have my stomach pumped.

3:00 P.M.   Arrive back at camp.

3:30 P.M.   Leave camp to kill deer.

4:00 P.M.   Return to camp for bullets.

4:01 P.M.	Load gun. Leave camp again.
5:00 P.M.	Empty gun on squirrel that is bugging me.
6:00 P.M.	Arrive in camp. See deer grazing in camp.
6:01 P.M.	Load gun.
6:02 P.M.	Fire gun.
6:03 P.M.	One dead pickup.
6:05 P.M.	Partner arrives in camp dragging deer.
6:06 P.M.	Repress desire to shoot hunting partner.
6:07 P.M.	Fall into fire.
6:10 P.M.	Change clothes.
6:15 P.M.	Take pickup. Leave hunting partner and his deer in camp.
6:25 P.M.	Pickup boils over — hole shot in block.
6:26 P.M.	Start walking.
6:30 P.M.	Stumble and fall. Drop gun in the mud.
6:45 P.M.	Meet bear.
6:36 P.M.	Take aim.
6:37 P.M.	Fire gun, blow up barrel plugged with mud.
6:38 P.M.	Mess pants.
6:39 P.M.	Climb tree.
9:00 P.M.	Bear leaves. Wrap !?%$# gun around tree.
Midnight	Home at last.
Sunday	Watch football game on TV, slowly tearing up hunting license into small pieces.

Bowhunter Belly Crawls To Trophy Whitetail

John Schnider

To say I plan my hunt would be an understatement. I eat, sleep and breathe deer. It is a way of life for me. There isn't a day that goes by that I am not thinking of how I can outwit a mature buck. I guess you could say it's an obsession. Just when you think you have a particular buck figured out, he will do something to make you look like a total fool.

I am fortunate enough to work for my father who is an avid deer hunter with many years of experience under his belt. So he understands why I frequently need to take time off.

This past hunting season was my best deer season so far. I put in literally hundreds of hours in hunting time. From all of my preseason scouting and a few super nice shed horns I found, I was really excited about the prospects, but my season, like most, was filled with highs and lows. There were occasions when I failed to capitalize on a few super nice bucks.

Because I hunt only with a bow and arrow, the shooting distance is limited. I shoot totally instinctively with an 82-pound Jennings compound with 2219 Easton arrows tipped with 125-grain Thunderheads.

The rut had come and gone and it was December 17. We had just gotten the biggest snowstorm of the year a couple of days earlier. Everything was covered with 12 inches of snow. This particular spot that I hunt is an overgrown cow pasture. It is sparsely covered with big oak trees intermingled with a variety of pines. The contour of the land is gently rolling with the hilltops completely bare and valleys choked with wild rose bushes (a jungle of thorns!).

I got to my hunting spot extra early that morning because I knew it would take me longer in the boot deep snow to reach my stand. As I was walking in the predawn stillness, I saw a falling star. Now I'm not one who believes in superstition but what the heck! I don't think I have to tell you what my wish was.

Only after screwing in the metal tree steps did I sense the cold. Carefully I climbed up to my lofty perch. It would still be a little while until good light. I got situated and waited.

Although I had on several layers of clothes, the cold was slowly creeping into my bones. There was a crisp, steady wind making matters even worse. I was pressed up against

continued on page 172

the trunk of the tree using it as a windbreak, when I saw a dark object coming toward me. Only after I wiped away frozen tears caused by the bone chilling wind, could I tell it was a little basket racked buck. As the little buck fed on past me, I listened to a couple of owls hooting back and forth to each other with an almost mesmerizing effect.

I wondered if I was even going to harvest a deer this year. I had only seven days left to hunt until I had to leave town to visit relatives for the remainder of the season. I had set my standards high and had let some really respectable bucks go by earlier in the season. I thought to myself, "Was it all worth it?"

The sun was just barely visible above the horizon when a group of five does came trotting by. They were nervous about something. They would run a little way and then stop and watch their back trail. I was hoping that one of the yearling does was coming into heat late and they were running from a persistent buck. No such luck. As I waited for another hour without seeing anything, my enthusiasm rapidly dwindled. I decided to get down and do some still hunting. I wanted to check out the upper end of the pasture.

I keep a log from every time I go scouting or hunting. Before this hunt I had check my notes from previous years to see what the deer were doing in this area at this time under similar conditions. I had found out that the last time there was this much snow, the deer were feeding heavily on the upper pasture. Most of the wild rose briars are there. They eat the berries off the briars because they are off the ground and easily accessible.

I climbed down from the tree and removed some clothes, since I was dressed for sitting, not walking around in the deep snow. I had just finished stuffing the extra clothing in my backpack and had put my snow camouflage back on when two bucks suddenly appeared.

I stood perfectly still as they closed the distance. At 10 feet, the lead buck came to an abrupt halt. He stopped so suddenly that the second buck ran into him. They both stared holes through me. Finally their nerves got the better of them and with the stiff legged gait a whitetail uses when he's not sure what's wrong, they trotted off.

The sun continued to climb into the morning sky as I quietly walked into the brisk wind. About halfway there, I spotted a small doe headed in my direction. I concealed myself in a small clump of crab apple trees. As soon as she got downwind and got a whiff of me, she headed for parts unknown.

There was one briar patch in particular I wanted to check. I had seen deer there several times before. It is located on the side of a small hill. Ever so cautiously, I made my way to the crest of the hill. I peered over the top. The briars were full of deer. I dropped to my knees to reduce the chance of being spotted. After closer observation, I could see it was the same deer I had seen at the other end of the pasture.

The change of events that occurred next will be etched in my mind forever. Picture this, if you can! I'm looking through a set of binoculars at the twin bucks in the same field of view. All of a sudden a gigantic set of antlers appears, completely blocking out the twin bucks!

In total disbelief, I lowered the binoculars to see if I was dreaming. Had I wanted to see a big buck so bad that my mind was playing tricks on me? Could this be for real? I was almost afraid to look for fear that nothing would be there. But, sure enough, between me and the smaller bucks, was a massive set of antlers, bobbing up and down as the buck was feeding. The briars were so thick and as he was standing in a slight depression, the only think I could see was his rack.

continued on page 174

Instantly, I broke out in a cold sweat. My mind was going ten different directions at once. "Do this! Do that! Don't do this! Don't do that!"

The only thing between me and the briar patch was about 70 yards of wide open, snow covered ground. As long as the deer stayed in the briars, I had a slim chance of getting closer.

I stepped off my back pack so I could move more freely. I then belly crawled through the deep snow, carefully closing the distance. While in the prone position, I would stop every few feet and glass, making sure that my presence was still undetected. Shortly before I reached the briars, I removed my binoculars to avoid potential interference with my shot. I then removed my left glove which had become coated with ice during my approach, making it impossible to keep a firm grip on the bow.

Luckily, I made it to the edge of the briars unnoticed. As I raised to a kneeling position, I nocked an arrow. No shot was available. It was too thick. The only thing I could do was wait and pray that the wind wouldn't switch. At this point, my nerves were frayed to say the least. Again, my subconscious took over. "Should I stand and try to shoot through the thick briars? Would the wind change and he'd be gone forever?"

I had put in many hard hours waiting for a chance at a buck of this caliber. Now was not the time to make a foolish mistake.

After minutes that seemed like forever, I could see the outline of his body. He was feeding closer! He turned and offered a broadside shot at 15 yards. It took all the will power I could ever hope to have to keep from shooting. There were still too many briars in the way.

Then as if on cue, he took a few steps forward, exposing himself ever so slightly. My instincts as a bowhunter took control. In one fluid motion, I stood, picked a spot, drew and released.

On impact, deer scattered in all directions. The buck lunged forward, ripping through the briars like they were not even there. At 30 yards, he stopped in a wide open clearing and was looking back over his shoulder. I was positive I had connected with my shot but there were no visible signs of a wound. I couldn't believe he was just standing there. All I could think of was that this magnificent buck was going to get away! I couldn't take my eyes off his rack.

I then proceeded to bounce a second arrow off his antlers. As he took off running, my whole season flashed before my eyes. Hundreds of hours wasted!

He ran about 40 yards when all of a sudden, he dropped to his knees. I thought he had tripped on something. He then fell over on his side, kicked one time and laid there, completely motionless. I couldn't believe what I was seeing. "Was he dead? Did I really get him?"

I wanted to run right over to him. Instead, I circled around in front, just in case. By this time, I could see his face buried in the snow. I knew it was over. I felt like screaming, "He's mine!"

With a 21⅝-inch inside spread and 10 evenly matched tines, he officially scored 161⅛ Boone and Crockett points. My first shot had passed completely through his heart and both lungs.

Most hunters might not think of this hunt as a once in a lifetime experience. I do. I didn't travel thousands of miles to hunt the unmistakable king of the wild, the brown bear, or spend my life savings and plan for several years to hunt some of the most breathtaking and treacherous country in the world in hopes of bagging the elusive Dall sheep. This hunt took place in my home state of Illinois, hunting what is to me the most cunning and craftiest big game animal there is, the whitetail deer.

"Take the penalty!"

Write Your Own Story

Here's a game you can do with one or more of your buddies. First, have someone give you a word for each of these categories. Then, read the story below out loud, putting their words in at where indicated.

#1 noun (any object, animal etc.): ＿＿＿＿＿＿＿＿＿＿

#2 tool: ＿＿＿＿＿＿＿＿＿＿＿＿＿＿＿＿＿

#3 past-tense verb (like jumped, coughed etc.): ＿＿＿＿＿

#4 food: ＿＿＿＿＿＿＿＿＿＿＿＿＿＿＿＿＿＿

#5 article of clothing: ＿＿＿＿＿＿＿＿＿＿＿＿＿

#6 sound or noise: ＿＿＿＿＿＿＿＿＿＿＿＿＿＿

#7 animal: ＿＿＿＿＿＿＿＿＿＿＿＿＿＿＿＿＿

#8 body part: ＿＿＿＿＿＿＿＿＿＿＿＿＿＿＿＿

#9 name of friend or famous person: ＿＿＿＿＿＿＿＿

I was walking through the woods last fall when I heard a noise in a tree. I looked up, and saw that there was a (#1 noun here) up in the branches! I sure was surprised, and I decided it needed to be brought down. I raised my (#2 tool here) to my shoulder and (#3 verb here) hard. Nothing happened, so I decided to take a break and figure out what to do about it. I sat down on a stump and pulled some (#4 food here) out of my pocket and polished that off. Well, the sun was pretty warm, so I took off my (#5 article of clothing here). Between the food and the warm sun, I got kind of sleepy, and pretty soon I dozed off. A while later, I was awakened by a (#6 sound here) in the woods. I jumped up to see what it was, and just as I did, the (#1 noun here) fell out of the tree and landed on my head! Next thing I knew, a (#7 animal here) came by to check out the racket. It didn't know what to make of the situation, so it grabbed my (#8 body part here) and started tugging real hard! Lucky for me, though, (#9 name here) came by and helped me get out of the mess I was in. Boy, you never know what will happen when you go for a walk in the woods!

That Place Is Haunted

Michael D. Faw

I was bowhunting white-tailed deer in the Appalachian Mountains in western NC as the leaves were turning their brilliant fall colors. The red maple leaves and the yellow poplar leaves made the hills look alive with the bright colors.The leaves were just starting to fall from the trees and allow better viewing of the steep mountains and ridges.

On this particular hunt I was hunting with a relatively new bowhunter who was several years younger than I. He relied on my every word about deer and how to bowhunt. We were hunting a new area and staying in his uncle's cabin in Allegheny County. I found some terrific deer sign, a few old apple trees and places where plenty of deer were sliding under fences to enter nearby fields. The trails were well worn and the deer were plentiful.

I decided to do a little scouting and walked into a region I had never been in before. While walking the fenceline I saw an old homestead down in the valley below me and went to investigate. The home was abandoned, run down and weathered gray. It looked just like the home that the famous Jason from the "Friday the 13th" horror series had lived in and where he had killed several victims in the horror film. The resemblance was pretty scary even for me and I knew my hunting partner had seen the movie. He had even confided that parts of the horror film had really scared him. I had found his weak spot and would set up the ultimate joke.

I did find a good deer trail on the fence line just up the hill from the house. Maybe even the deer were afraid to travel close to this place! That evening in the cabin I told my friend he should hunt the new hot deer trail I had discovered, he would surely get a deer there. I somehow overlooked telling him about the eerie house that would be in front of him in the valley.

We headed out before daylight the next morning and I located the fence. I then told my friend how much further down to go until he would find the deer trail and a noticeable tree to place his stand in. There was an eerie fog in the area, perfect conditions! I went to another area to hunt.

I came back to our cabin at lunchtime and found my friend white-as-a-ghost and on the couch inside. He blurted out I had not scouted the area too well. He then relayed how he found the trail and the tree, then erected his stand and waited for the deer to come along. However, as the light increased he saw this ominous ghost house appearing the valley in front of him and through the fog. He stated the lighter the day became, the scarier the house looked. He commented he thought he saw "Jason" standing in the window with an ax! He was only there long enough to get his stand out of the tree and had ran back to the cabin. He never even hunted that morning, the haunted house had truly upset him.

I got a good laugh out of the scare the place had given him. After that incident he was reluctant to hunt areas I scouted for him unless he went along and did a thorough check of the area.

The Legend of the Madstone

The same process that creates pearls from an irritant in an oyster is supposedly responsible for creating a healing stone in the stomach of a deer. These "madstones" are alleged to cure rabies victims.

The calcium formed stone is also supposed to counteract infections and poisons, according to the legend.

The best ones come from the rumen, or fore stomach, of a deer. The stone is known as a *bezoar*, a Persian word meaning the explosion of poison.

Although today's doctors don't put much faith in these madstones, there are a number of reports of people being saved from rabid animal bites. Nowadays, the doctors say those animals probably didn't really have rabies to begin with and the bit person was not really in danger.

According to the legend, the madstone needed to rest on the wound until it would no longer stick, at which time the patient was healed.

179

Chewing Can Be Hazardous To Your Health

NAHC Member's Story

Charles L. Lusk

I have hunted since I was 10 years old. After taking some 30 whitetail, mule deer and elk, and hunting turkey for three years, you would think I would be able to control the excitement felt when game is sighted. Not so!

It was opening morning of the 1979 gun season. I had thoroughly scouted the 1,200 acre lease our club held in the deer-rich Piedmont section of Georgia, and knew I had selected the best stand to ambush a good buck using the area.

Perched 20 feet above the ground, the morning fog thickening to soup, I stuffed a liberal amount of "Red Man" into my cheek. The chew had just gotten to the good part, putting out copious amounts of juice, when I noticed a shadow floating out of the fog 40 yards away.

I froze. Deer? Nope. A flock of turkeys fed slowly through the mist to gather underneath my stand. 13 hens and young. Fearing any movement would spook the turkeys and any deer nearby, I remained still, with my mouth so full of tobacco juice I could hardly hold it all.

As my pulse and blood pressure pounded to high levels because of a flock that near (any turkey hunter knows what I mean), I noticed another shadow moving in from the side. An eight-point buck, obviously curious, had his attention riveted on the turkeys.

With visions of his horns hanging on my wall, I began to

ease my rifle into place. A big hen, directly under my stand, jerked fully erect, and let out the warning "putt." The flock disappeared almost instantly. The buck turned inside out and was gone in two jumps. I was so startled by the sudden change of events, I swallowed the tobacco juice, which had by then built up to a good half pint.

The foggy pine woods had grown immediately quiet, broken only by my gagging, sputtering and spitting. The thought did cross my mind that to fall out of the stand and land on my head might be a better alternative to continuing the agony going on in my churning stomach, burning throat, swimming head and watering eyes.

A half hour later, when I could move without feeling the urge to throw up, I climbed down from the stand and wobbled back to camp, vowing a change to less potent chewing gum.

"...Well...he was going hunting but his car wouldn't start..."

Hunting Trip Log #1

One of the most important things we get from hunting is the memories. We all enjoy re-living our favorite hunting trips, whether with family and friends, or just in our own minds. Use these pages to preserve the details in writing, and you'll always remember the success stories and memorable events. This Trip Log is easy to use and contains basic information about your hunt: where you hunted, who you were with, a record of success, and other fun-to-remember highlights.

Dates: _____ Location: _____

Companions: _____

Outfitter/Guide: _____

Species Hunted: _____

Weapons Used: _____ Ammo: _____

_____ Ammo: _____

_____ Ammo: _____

Big Game Trophies Taken By Our Group

Animal	Sex	Weight	Rack Size	Hunter	Date/Time

Weather Conditions: _____

Small Game Taken By Our Group

Species	Males	Females	Hunter	Date/Time

Trip Highlights

Best Trophy: _____

Best Shot: _____

Most Successful Hunter: _____

Got Skunked: _____

Best Camp Cook: _____ Cooked Worst Meal: _____

New Hunters in Camp: _____

Hunting Trip Log #2

Dates: _____ Location: _____
Companions: _____
Outfitter/Guide: _____
Species Hunted: _____
Weapons Used: _____ Ammo: _____
_____ Ammo: _____
_____ Ammo: _____

Big Game Trophies Taken By Our Group

Animal	Sex	Weight	Rack Size	Hunter	Date/Time

Weather Conditions: _____

Small Game Taken By Our Group

Species	Males	Females	Hunter	Date/Time

Trip Highlights

Best Trophy: _____
Best Shot: _____
Most Successful Hunter: _____
Got Skunked: _____
Best Camp Cook: _____ Cooked Worst Meal: _____
New Hunters in Camp: _____

Answers to The Great Whitetail Quiz

The quiz is divided into eight parts. To score your whitetail knowledge, give yourself one point for each correct answer, then total the points for all eight parts.

90–97 points   You're a whitetail wizard!
80–89 points: Above average
70–79 points: Average
60–69 points: Below average
Below 60 points: Deer dunce.

Part One questions on pages 18-19:

1) A	5) D	9) C
2) B	6) B	10) B
3) A	7) A	11) B
4) D	8) C	12) A

Part Two questions on pages 44-45:

13) A	18) A	23) B
14) B	19) C	24) A
15) A	20) D	25) B
16) A	21) C	
17) B	22) D	

Part Three questions on pages 66-67:

26) A	29) A	32) B
27) B	30) B	33) C
28) A	31) C	34) B

Part Four questions on pages 78-79:

35) C	41) B	47) C
36) A	42) D	48) A
37) A	43) A	49) B
38) C	44) A	50) A
39) B	45) B	
40) B	46) A	

Part Five questions on pages 110-111:

51) B	55) C	59) A
52) D	56) D	60) B
53) C	57) A	61) A
54) B	58) B	62) C

Part Six questions on pages 136-137:

63) C	68) A	73) C
64) C	69) C	74) B
65) A	70) B	75) B
66) B	71) A	
67) C	72) B	

Part Seven questions on pages 144-145:

76) B	82) B
77) B	83) A
78) A	84) B
79) C	85) A
80) B	86) B
81) B	87) B

Part Eight questions on pages 164:

88) A	95) B
89) A	96) B
90) B	97) B
91) B	
92) A	
93) B	
94) A	

Word Search Answers

Knife Makers, page 23:

```
U K C U B S W E S T E R N E
C A N O T G N I M E R R E K
W H R W E N H A F R O S T C
N K E A S P Y D E R C O D A
C R K H E S A C L I V N W J
A A O S T G Y L O I U I R K
M M B R K I A N C I N F E C
I H U E C K M T S C E C G A
L C S K O G O B H H A O E L
L N R T P R M E P E L R B
U E A N I I S R U R N O B G
S B S N T T O M A E L N E N
S S O P E A A R I E N I R G
L X B R O W N I N G B A N Y
E S A S E L B R A M F L E E
```

Archery, page 51:

```
P R A D C T I D R A U G M R A
C E O R E F F R T T E D S N U
S E E A V Q F A N T H N T E R
I G L W R U O W I H E U A T G
A R B L U I T W O R S O B O N
W W A E C V E E P S A P I K I
A B C N E E L I G E E M L E H
R O P G R R Y G N O L O I U C
D W R T B O W H I T E C Z U T
R S N H C E D T K R R G E A E
E T R A N H W A C Q I W R T L
V R M T S E R W O R R A E D F
O I F S H A F T N N L L I M B
O N P I R G Z R H I S I G H T
T G W O R R A E D E L E E H W
```

Big Gun Word Search, page 114:

The Deer Woods, page 149:

Animal Match-Ups Answers (page 27)

1. Bighorn Sheep
2. Black Bear
3. Caribou
4. Antelope
5. Blue-Winged Teal
6. Javelina
7. Wild Turkey
8. Elk
9. Moose
10. Ring-Necked Pheasant
11. Ruffed Grouse
12. Canvasback
13. Woodcock
14. Squirrel
15. Canada Goose
16. Whitetail Deer

Crossword Answers

All About Deer, page 33:

Bird Hunting, page 42:

Crossword Answers

Take Your Best "Shot," page 93:

The Hunt, page 156:

Answers to The "Bear Necessities" (page 37)

Black Bear   Grizzly Bear   Polar Bear

Answers to Know Your Knives! (page 68)

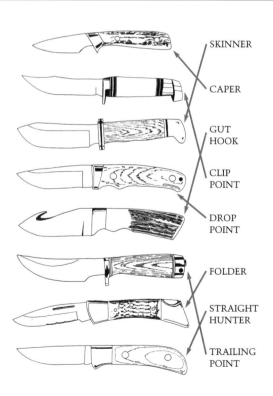

SKINNER

CAPER

GUT HOOK

CLIP POINT

DROP POINT

FOLDER

STRAIGHT HUNTER

TRAILING POINT

Answers to Name That Track (pages 76-66)

SQUIRREL | BADGER

BEAVER

RACCOON

RABBIT

FOX | LYNX | SKUNK | PORCUPINE

COYOTE

Answers to Name That Cartridge (page 101)

1- .22
2- .223 Remington
3- .243 Winchester
4- .270 Winchester
5- .30-30
6- .30-06 Springfield
7- .7mm Remington Magnum
8- .300 Weatherby Magnum
9- .338 Winchester Magnum
10- .375 Holland and Holland

Answers to Shoot Straight (page 119)

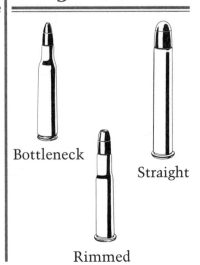

Bottleneck

Straight

Rimmed

Answers to How Well Do You Know The Basics? (page 131)

1. It obviously depends on the circumstances, such as where the animal was hit, the weather and hours of daylight remaining. A good rule of thumb, however, is to wait at least one hour before starting to trail.
2. All of the above. Animals often double back on a trail or stagger off regular trails before dying. You may need to try all available options to locate your game.
3. True.
4. False; this is an exception to the rule. If the animal is kept walking the would may stay open.
5. Either C or D. Bubbles may indicate a neck hit where the neck arteries and windpipe have been hit.
6. Liver or kidney.
7. Field dress it. To keep the meat from spoiling it's important to remove the entrails as soon as possible.

Answers to Super Slam (page 142)

Here's the Super Slam list every hunter dreams of bagging!

1. Pronghorn Antelope
2. Alaska Brown Bear
3. Black Bear
4. Grizzly Bear
5. Polar Bear
6. Bison
7. Barren Ground Caribou
8. Mountain Caribou
9. Quebec-Labrador Caribou
10. Woodland Caribou
11. Cougar
12. Columbia Blacktail Deer
13. Coues' Whitetail Deer
14. Mule Deer
15. Sitka Blacktail Deer
16. Whitetail Deer
17. American Elk
18. Roosevelt's Elk
19. Rocky Mountain Goat
20. Alaska-Yukon Moose
21. Canada Moose
22. Wyoming Moose
23. Muskox
24. Bighorn Sheep
25. Dall's Sheep
26. Desert Sheep
27. Stone's Sheep

ATTENTION CLUB MEMBERS:

The North American Hunting Club is already putting together next year's *Huntin' Camp Tales* book. We want to publish your best hunting jokes and stories in next year's edition!

Here's how it works: Just write down your favorite hunting joke or story, attach it to the completed form below and send it in to the club.

We're looking for anything funny, unique or exciting– everything and anything you'd like to share with your fellow club Members. Send them in – if your entry is used, we'll print your name, city and state right along with your story or joke. You'll be famous, and we'll even send you a FREE copy of the book.

Write down your hunting stories, jokes, observations or anything you'd like to share and send to:

North American Hunting Club *Huntin' Camp Tales* Book
12301 Whitewater Drive
Minnetonka, MN 55343

Don't wait! Let us hear from you today!

Copy this page and send along with your entry.
Be sure to fill out the information below.

Name_____

Address _____

City_____ State _____ Zip _____

Member # _____

*I authorize the NAHC to reproduce my submission in their upcoming **Huntin' Camp Tales** book. I agree that NAHC may edit this piece if needed.*

Signature_____ Date _____